AIR FRYER COOKBOOK

Easy, Healthy Recipes for Beginners (Vol.1)

CLARISSA HEWITT

Sommario

Introduction

We all know it, and you are here because you know it too; eating healthy is not only a fad choice but an entire change to your lifestyle and state of mind. Each day you must strive to make good decisions and take baby steps towards your fitness goals. Slowly but surely, you seem to create healthy habits that stick. But in the world, we live in today, there is literally temptation around every corner. From the candy bowl at work to the restaurant menu to the fast food joint perfectly stationed on your commute home, it is hard to say no to such delicious enticements. So, how is one supposed to fortify themselves to stay on track? We will tackle some of the best tips to assist you in achieving your fitness goals, whether you wish to shed some excess fat or are just wanting to look and feel a bit better, there is always a way to shield yourself against unhealthy temptations.

Eat before you go

It is difficult to make healthy decisions when your stomach is growling. Make sure you eat before you head to work, to the store, or anywhere where you might be led to make a poor choice in food. Or, take a healthy snack with you. If you are always letting yourself get to the point of "hangry-ness," you are blatantly setting yourself up to feast in the land of junk foods. It is also important to eat consistent meals throughout the day to help you stay on track as well. Learn to cook in the comfort of your own home instead of wasting your hard-earned money on food that really doesn't suit you well.

Plan ahead

It is in your best interest to be prepared. Start each week by making yourself a meal plan. List what you need and make it a goal to stick as close as you can to this plan. This will help you to reduce the number of times you go to the store, which results in a decrease of impulsive buys.

Plan for dining out too! Many restaurants now post their entire menu online for customers to look at. Know what options they have available, which will make it easier to make healthier decisions.

Trick what triggers you

All of us have a version of kryptonite, those delicious but bad-for-you eats that leave us feeling helpless and unable to fight back. Keep these sorts of temptations out of sight and out of mind, or better yet, out of your home and office altogether. To stay the course of becoming a healthier version of yourself, you must learn the importance of making decisions when confronted with healthier alternatives to what you are triggered by to counteract them. For example, if you are like me, ice cream is always a losing battle. Instead of heading to scoop some mint chocolate chip that is loaded with sugar and countless calories, opt to make a healthier version, such as Banana Ice Cream!

Investigate cravings

When you find yourself in a hankering for something unsavory for your body, take a moment to stop and ask yourself why you are craving a certain item. What is it that you are craving? There are many of us, myself included, that mix up our emotional cravings with food, and sadly, food will never fill this type of void.If you are always falling for some sort of temptation, look inside yourself and consider what your energy is like and what you are feeling and thinking at that moment. People are more prone to unhealthy and overeating when they are stressed out, tired, anxious, bored, or trying to cope with an uncertain situation. Instead of using food to cope, evaluate your emotional status and see how you can resolve the negativity that is fueling your bad choice making when it comes to what you eat and what you crave.

Create a path to success

Make it a priority to keep up with a food journal. Track what you eat, how you feel when you eat items, what makes you crave certain things, etc. Often, simply jotting down a terrible choice of food can lead you to make much better decisions in the future.

You can also write out mantras in this journal as well. Make up a phrase you can easily remember that will help you to find the motivation to keep moving forward in a healthy pattern.

"I'm worth it."

"I am striving for ultimate health."

"I am in control of the choices I make."

Act on "give-ins" in moderation

It is perfectly fine to give in and succumb to our favorite junk foods that ultimately satisfy our taste buds on occasion. Make sure to write down your cravings in your food journal. I like to tell people to eat for fuel 90% of the time and eat for fun 10%!

Don't stop

Don't let an occasional slip-up detour you from sticking to your goal of becoming a healthier version of yourself. We are all human and make mistakes.

Don't get all caught up in eating something unhealthy and ruin your day because of it. You have the control to turn that once unhealthy day into a very healthy one.

Let carbs fight for you

Anti-carb attitudes are wildly outdated. Research has shown how carbohydrates that are packed with resistant starches can help you to feel more satisfied and promote overall satiety. It takes energy to break down these starches and causes a decrease in insulin spikes compared to "bad carbs."

Believe it or not, carbs are essential to the weight loss game. If you eat more healthy carbs and avoid the processed ones, you are giving your body the energy source it needs and prefers, which provides you with the ultimate mental satisfaction you need to keep pushing forward.

Get grateful

When you are famished, and at home alone, it can be very tempting to grab that bag of mini donuts to nom on instead of picking a piece of fruit. Before you decide on s snack, take a moment to pause and appreciate. Ponder over how hard it is to grow produce to eat, how much you enjoy the natural juiciness of biting into an orange, or walking to the farmers market. Can you say any of these things about that bag of mini donuts you were about to devour?

Gratitude is one of those off-key things that can ultimately help you in your weight loss and fitness journey. You are taking a second to find the foods that bring your nourishment, which is a lot harder to come by with processed eats. This helps in the decision process of making thoughtful choices.

Don't fear these foods

Despite what many people think and what you have read time after time, the following foods at great if you are striving for a finer waistline! Cereal and milk: While there are many cereals out there that are packed with excess sugars with barely any nutritional value, there are many others that have 2 ½ grams of fiber per serving. Eat these types with 8 ounces of whole milk to feel satisfied in the morning. Opt for cereals that have 10 grams or less of sugar per serving. If you are hankering for additional sweetness, eat a piece of fruit! Greek yogurt: Opt for whole-milk Greek yogurt, and you will get a healthy source of fat that satiates you! Eating high-fat dairy items can help in lowering the risk of becoming overweight by 8%.

Dried fruits: While many people think that dried fruit is as bad for you as gummy candies are, this is simply not true. While you should never overeat dried fruit, these are not packed with added sugars and is denser in calories than raw fruit. Loaded with vitamins and fiber, it can make a great snack in moderation.

White potatoes: Known for their high carbohydrate content, many people try their best to avoid white potatoes. But it isn't their carb content as much as it is the forms we eat them in. From potato chips to fries drizzled with butter, it is no wonder these below ground veggies have gotten a bad rap. Potatoes, when not covered in processed things, are packed with potassium, full of vitamins and are relatively low in calorie count. They are good carbs and increase overall satiety.

Don't force foods you hate on yourself

Do not feel bad if you are not with your friends and coworkers on hopping on the newest and latest diet fads. This certainly does not mean you are on the wrong track. If there are certain foods you do not like and appreciate, then don't force yourself to eat them. This will only detour you from sticking to your health goals. It will leave you more unsatisfied than before, and you will feel less nourished.

What is an Air Fryer?

The air fryer is a relatively new kitchen appliance used to fry foods with a little oil. An air fryer is the direct counterpart of the traditional frying pan, oven, and multi-cooker. With an air fryer, you use hot air instead of frying oil to cook dishes. With an air fryer, you can bake, roast, grill, and fry. You only need to use a little oil for baking, frying, roasting, and grilling. The air fryer heats the air to a temperature of around 400 degrees Fahrenheit. The hot air constantly circulates through the pan, enabling you to cook dishes evenly all around. This cooks all sides equally and creates a crispy crust.

Function Keys

- Button / Play/Pause Button
  - o This Play/Pause button allows you to pause during the middle of the cooking so you can shake the air fryer basket or flip the food to ensure it cooks evenly.
- -/+ Button /Minus/Plus Button
  - o This button is used to change the time or temperature.
- Keep Warm
  - o This function keeps your food warm for 30 minutes.
- Food Presets
  - o This button gives you the ability to cook food without second-guessing. The time and temperature are already set, so new users find this setting useful.
- Roast or Broil
  - o You can roast or broil with this setting. When using a conventional oven, you need to brown the meat before roasting. You can skip this step when cooking with an air fryer.
- Dehydrate
  - o This setting cooks and dries food at a low temperature for a few hours. With this option, you can create your own beef jerky or dried fruit.
- Features of Your Air Fryer
  - o Portable: The cooking device is portable. The air fryer is designed to be easily transferred from your kitchen storage cabinet to the countertop or elsewhere
- Automatic temperature control: You get perfectly cooked food every time with an air fryer.
  - o Digital touch screen: You don't have to learn complicated cooking skills, simplicity is inbuilt with an air fryer. With a few taps on the touch panel's screen, you can cook a variety of foods.

o   Timer and buzzer: No need to worry about overcooking your food. The timer and buzzer will let you know when your food is cooked.

Benefits of an Air Fryer

Reduces fat content: One-reason air fryers are better than deep fryers is the fact that they help cut down on fat. When you deep-fry your meals, the fat content in your food is very high because it requires immersing your food in oil. However, air fryers allow you to fry your food with little oil. This helps to reduce the fat content in your meal. Helps you lose weight: Air fryers are really good for weight loss. Aside from lowering the fat content in your meal, air fryers also help you reduce your calorie intake. The air fryer requires very little oil to make your food crispy and crunchy, thereby reducing your calorie intake. When deep-frying food in oil, we add many calories, so one of the most attractive benefits of an air fryer is the reduction of these extra calories. Lowers your consumption of harmful compounds: Deep fried foods contain a chemical called acrylamide content. This chemical is hardly ever present in air-fried meals. Much healthier than deep-fried foods: If you desire to eat healthy meals, join the number of people who have made air-fryer meals their lifestyle. Reduction in cooking time: With the programming of temperature and time, you can control the constant flow of hot air and accelerate the process of cooking food. It could save up to 40% of the time used in a regular frying process.

Reduction of energy expenditure: If you compare the energy consumption of the air fryer with that of a standard electric oven, you can see consumption varies by a reasonably high percentage. You can save more than 50% of electrical energy when using the fryer. For example, the air fryer consumes about 390Wh to fry a pound of potatoes, 45% less electricity than a conventional oven uses. Saving money: You use less oil, and you need less energy when cooking with an air fryer. So you save money. Easy to clean: The cleaning is easier with an air fryer. The container where the food is placed is removable, which makes it easy to wash and clean. Saves space: You can save kitchen space when using an air fryer.

Air Fryer vs. Deep Fryer

Oil usage: Air fryers use less oil, this means using an air fryer costs you less. You need to use a lot more oil when deep-frying. Although you can reuse the oil, most health experts do not recommend it. Healthy cooking: Fried foods such as air fried French fries contain up to 80% less fat in comparison to deep-fried French fries. Cleaning: Compared to a deep fryer, cleaning an air fryer is easy. You need to clean the deep fryer and the oil vapor that settles on the kitchen walls and countertop. Safety: An air fryer is safe to use. With a deep fryer, there is always a risk of accidents. Multiple uses: You can only fry in a deep-fryer. On the other hand, you can cook in many different ways in an air fryer.

Air Fryer vs. Convection Oven

Less hazardous: An air fryer gives you a one-stop cooking solution. With ovens, you often must cook food in a pan for a few minutes to bring out the color and aromas before putting it in the oven.

Safe: You can open and close the air fryer without the risk of burning yourself. A traditional oven presents a risk of fire.

Time: You can cook faster in an air fryer.

Cleaning: Cleaning your air fryer is easy. On the other hand, cleaning an oven is time-consuming.

Frequently Asked Questions

Q: Can I cook different foods in the air fryer?

A: Yes, you can cook different foods in your air fryer. You can use it for cooking different types of foods like casseroles and even desserts.

Q: How much food can I put inside?

A: Different air fryers tend to have different capacities. To know how much food you can put in, look for the "max" mark and use it as a guide to filling the basket.

Q: Can I add ingredients during the cooking process?

A: Yes, you can. Just open the air fryer and add ingredients. There is no need to change the internal temperature as it will stabilize once you close the air fryer chamber.

Q: Can I put aluminum or baking paper at the bottom of the air fryer?

A: Yes, you can use both to line the base of the air fryer. However, make sure that you poke holes so that the hot air can pass through the material and allow the food to cook.

Q: Do I need to preheat?

A: Preheating the air fryer can reduce the cooking time. However, if you forgot to preheat, it is still okay. To preheat the air fryer, simply set it to the cooking temperature and set the timer for 5 minutes. Once the timer turns off, place your food in the basket and continue cooking.

Tips for the Perfect Air Fry

Find a place in your kitchen where it will always be easy to access the air fryer, to the point that you simply need to open the cooking container and add your ingredients.

Different recipes require different temperatures to ensure that the food is cooked properly. Follow the recipe as precisely as possible to ensure that your food tastes delicious.

Aluminum foil helps with cleaning and is often used to add even more gradual control to the cooking process for the ingredients.

Add a dash of water when cooking fatty foods. You will notice a small drawer at the bottom of your air fryer. This is where you can add a splash of water when you are cooking foods that are high in fat. If the fat becomes too hot and drips to the bottom for too long, it can sometimes start to smoke. Adding vegetables prevents smoke. But if you are only cooking meat, then it is a good idea to add water to prevent the unpleasant smoke from rising.

Do not overcrowd the air fryer's cooking basket with too many ingredients. Make sure that the ingredients are all at one level, especially if you are preparing meat.

Flip foods halfway through the cooking time if you want both sides of your food to have a crispy coating.

Do not worry about opening the air fryer mid-cycle. Unlike other cooking methods, the air fryer doesn't lose heat intensity if you open it in the middle of cooking. Once you close the top again, the device will go back to cooking temperature and continue to cook the food.

There is a basket at the bottom of the air fryer to collect grease. If you take out both the cooking basket and the bottom basket at the same time and you tip them over, the grease from the bottom will be transferred onto your plate along with food. So, remove the bottom basket before serving the food.

Clean the air fryer after every use. Leftover food particles can turn into mold, develop bacteria, and cause unpleasant after-effects. To avoid this, clean the air fryer after every use.

Once you clean the air fryer, assemble everything. The air fryer will dry itself within a few minutes.

Here are some of the cooking techniques that you can use with this appliance:

Fry: You can avoid oil when cooking, but a small amount adds crunch and flavor to your food.

Roast: You can produce high quality roasted food in the air fryer

Bake: You can bake bread, cookies, and pastries.

Grill: You can effectively grill your food, no mess.

To start cooking, you just need to spray the fryer basket with some cooking spray or put in a little cooking oil, add the ingredients, and adjust the temperature and time.

Step-By-Step Air Frying

Air fryers work on Rapid Air Technology. The cooking chamber of the air fryer emits heat from a heating element that is close to the food. The exhaust fan that is present above the cooking chamber aids in the necessary airflow from the underside. For cooking using an air fryer, here are some steps that you need to follow:

1. Prepare Fried Foods:
2. Place the air fryer on a level and heatproof kitchen top.
3. Prepare the foods.
4. Grease the basket with a little oil and add a bit more to the food to avoid sticking.
5. If the food is marinated, pat it dry lightly to prevent splattering and excess smoke.
6. Use aluminum foil for easy cleaning.
7. Before Cooking:
8. Preheat the air fryer for 3 minutes before cooking.
9. Avoid overcrowding and leave sufficient space for air circulation.
10. During Cooking time:
11. Add water into the air fryer drawer to prevent excessive smoke and heat
12. Shake the basket or flip the food for even cooking at the halfway mark.
13. After Cooking:
14. Remove the basket from the drawer before taking out the food.
15. The juices in the air fryer drawer can be used to make delicious marinades and sauces
16. Unplug, cool, and then clean both the basket and drawer after use

Troubleshooting

Food not cooking perfectly: Follow the recipe exactly. Check whether or not you have overcrowded the ingredients. This is the main reason why food might not cook evenly in an air fryer.

White smoke: White smoke is usually the result of grease, so make sure that you have added some water to the bottom drawer to prevent the grease from overheating.

Black smoke: Black smoke is usually due to burnt food. You need to clean the air fryer after every use. If you do not, then the remaining food particles are burned when you use the appliance again. Turn the machine off and cool it completely. Then check it for burned food.

The appliance won't stop: The fan of the air fryer operates at high speed and needs some time to stop. Do not worry, it will stop soon.

- Cleaning Your Air Fryer
- Unplug the appliance and let it cool down.
- Wipe the outside with a damp cloth.
- Wash the basket, tray, and pan with hot water and soap. You can also use a dishwasher to wash these parts.
- Clean the inside of the air fryer with a damp cloth or sponge.
- Clean any food that is stuck to the heating element.

o   Dry the parts and assemble the air fryer.

Tips:

Use damp cloths to remove stuck-on food. Do not use utensils to avoid scratching the non-stick coating.

If the stuck-on food has hardened onto the basket or pan, then soak them in hot soapy water before trying to remove them.

Safety Tips

o   Do not buy a cheap, low-quality air fryer.
o   Do not place it on an uneven surface.
o   Do not overcrowd the basket.
o   Do not leave the appliance unattended.
o   Read the air fryer manual before using it.
o   Clean the appliance after every use.
o   Do not wash the electrical components.
o   Use the right amount of oil. Your air fryer needs only a little oil, so do not use extra.
o   Grease the air fryer basket. It will prevent food from getting stuck and prevent potential burning and smoking.
o   Dry your hands before touching the air fryer.
o   Make sure accessories are air fryer safe.
o   Shake the basket or flip the food during the middle of the cooking to ensure even cooking.
o   If your air fryer needs repairing, seek professional support.

Breakfast Recipes

1. Fluffy Cheesy Omelet

Preparation Time: 10 minutes
Cooking time: 15 minutes
Servings: 2
Ingredients:
4 eggs
1 large onion, sliced
1/8 cup cheddar cheese, grated
1/8 cup mozzarella cheese, grated
Cooking spray
¼ teaspoon soy sauce
Freshly ground black pepper, to taste
Directions:
Preheat the Air fryer to 360 o F and grease a pan with cooking spray.
Whisk together eggs, soy sauce and black pepper in a bowl.
Place onions in the pan and cook for about 10 minutes.
Pour the egg mixture over onion slices and top evenly with cheese.
Cook for about 5 more minutes and serve.
Nutrition:
Calories: 216, Fat: 13.8g, Carbohydrates: 7.9g, Sugar: 3.9g, Protein: 15.5g, Sodium: 251mg

2. Crust-Less Quiche

Preparation Time: 5 minutes
Cooking time: 30 minutes
Servings: 2
Ingredients:
4 eggs
¼ cup onion, chopped
½ cup tomatoes, chopped
½ cup milk
1 cup Gouda cheese, shredded
Salt, to taste
Directions:
Preheat the Air fryer to 340 o F and grease 2 ramekins lightly.
Mix together all the ingredients in a ramekin until well combined.
Place in the Air fryer and cook for about 30 minutes.
Dish out and serve.
Nutrition:
Calories: 348, Fat: 23.8g, Carbohydrates: 7.9g, Sugar: 6.3g, Protein: 26.1g, Sodium: 642mg

3. Milky Scrambled Eggs

Preparation Time: 10 minutes
Cooking time: 9 minutes

Servings: 2
Ingredients:
¾ cup milk
4 eggs
8 grape tomatoes, halved
½ cup Parmesan cheese, grated
1 tablespoon butter
Salt and black pepper, to taste
Directions:
Preheat the Air fryer to 360 o F and grease an Air fryer pan with butter.
Whisk together eggs with milk, salt and black pepper in a bowl.
Transfer the egg mixture into the prepared pan and place in the Air fryer.
Cook for about 6 minutes and stir in the grape tomatoes and cheese.
Cook for about 3 minutes and serve warm.
Nutrition:
Calories: 351, Fat: 22g, Carbohydrates: 25.2g, Sugar: 17.7g, Protein: 26.4g,
Sodium: 422mg

4. Toasties and Sausage in Egg Pond

Preparation Time: 10 minutes
Cooking time: 22 minutes
Servings: 2
Ingredients:
3 eggs
2 cooked sausages, sliced
1 bread slice, cut into sticks
1/8 cup mozzarella cheese, grated
1/8 cup Parmesan cheese, grated
¼ cup cream
Directions:
Preheat the Air fryer to 365 o F and grease 2 ramekins lightly.
Whisk together eggs with cream in a bowl and place in the ramekins.
Stir in the bread and sausage slices in the egg mixture and top with cheese.
Transfer the ramekins in the Air fryer basket and cook for about 22 minutes.
Dish out and serve warm.
Nutrition:
Calories: 261, Fat: 18.8g, Carbohydrates: 4.2g, Sugar: 1.3g, Protein: 18.3g, Sodium:
428mg

5. Banana Bread

Preparation Time: 10 minutes
Cooking time: 20 minutes
Servings: 8
Ingredients:
1 1/3 cups flour
1 teaspoon baking soda
1 teaspoon baking powder
½ cup milk
3 bananas, peeled and sliced

2/3 cup sugar

1 teaspoon ground cinnamon

1 teaspoon salt

½ cup olive oil

Directions:

Preheat the Air fryer to 330 o F and grease a loaf pan.

Mix together all the dry ingredients with the wet ingredients to form a dough.

Place the dough into the prepared loaf pan and transfer into an air fryer basket.

Cook for about 20 minutes and remove from air fryer.

Cut the bread into desired size slices and serve warm.

Nutrition:

Calories: 295, Fat: 13.3g, Carbohydrates: 44g, Sugar: 22.8g, Protein: 3.1g, Sodium: 458mg

6. Flavorful Bacon Cups

Preparation Time: 10 minutes

Cooking time: 15 minutes

Servings: 6

Ingredients:

6 bacon slices

6 bread slices

1 scallion, chopped

3 tablespoons green bell pepper, seeded and chopped

6 eggs

2 tablespoons low-fat mayonnaise

Directions:

Preheat the Air fryer to 375 o F and grease 6 cups muffin tin with cooking spray.

Place each bacon slice in a prepared muffin cup.

Cut the bread slices with round cookie cutter and place over the bacon slices.

Top with bell pepper, scallion and mayonnaise evenly and crack 1 egg in each muffin cup.

Place in the Air fryer and cook for about 15 minutes.

Dish out and serve warm.

Nutrition:

Calories: 260, Fat: 18g, Carbohydrates: 6.9g, Sugar: 1.03g, Protein: 16.7g, Sodium: 805mg

7. Crispy Potato Rosti

Preparation Time: 10 minutes

Cooking time: 15 minutes

Servings: 2

Ingredients:

½ pound russet potatoes, peeled and grated roughly

1 tablespoon chives, chopped finely

2 tablespoons shallots, minced

1/8 cup cheddar cheese

3.5 ounces smoked salmon, cut into slices

2 tablespoons sour cream

1 tablespoon olive oil

Salt and black pepper, to taste

Directions:

Preheat the Air fryer to 365 o F and grease a pizza pan with the olive oil.

Mix together potatoes, shallots, chives, cheese, salt and black pepper in a large bowl until well combined.

Transfer the potato mixture into the prepared pizza pan and place in the Air fryer basket.

Cook for about 15 minutes and dish out in a platter.

Cut the potato rosti into wedges and top with smoked salmon slices and sour cream to serve.

Nutrition:

Calories: 327, Fat: 20.2g, Carbohydrates: 23.3g, Sugar: 2.8g, Protein: 15.3g, Sodium: 316mg

8. Stylish Ham Omelet

Preparation Time: 10 minutes

Cooking time: 30 minutes

Servings: 2

Ingredients:

4 small tomatoes, chopped

4 eggs

2 ham slices

1 onion, chopped

2 tablespoons cheddar cheese

Salt and black pepper, to taste

Directions:

Preheat the Air fryer to 390 o F and grease an Air fryer pan.

Place the tomatoes in the Air fryer pan and cook for about 10 minutes.

Heat a nonstick skillet on medium heat and add onion and ham.

Stir fry for about 5 minutes and transfer into the Air fryer pan.

Whisk together eggs, salt and black pepper in a bowl and pour in the Air fryer pan.

Set the Air fryer to 335 o F and cook for about 15 minutes.

Dish out and serve warm.

Nutrition:

Calories: 255, Fat: 13.9g, Carbohydrates: 14.1g, Sugar: 7.8g, Protein: 19.7g, Sodium: 543mg

9. Healthy Tofu Omelet

Preparation Time: 10 minutes

Cooking time: 29 minutes

Servings: 2

Ingredients:

¼ of onion, chopped

12-ounce silken tofu, pressed and sliced

3 eggs, beaten

1 tablespoon chives, chopped

1 garlic clove, minced

2 teaspoons olive oil

Salt and black pepper, to taste

Directions:

Preheat the Air fryer to 355 o F and grease an Air fryer pan with olive oil.

Add onion and garlic to the greased pan and cook for about 4 minutes.

Add tofu, mushrooms and chives and season with salt and black pepper.

Beat the eggs and pour over the tofu mixture.

Cook for about 25 minutes, poking the eggs twice in between.

Dish out and serve warm.

Nutrition:

Calories: 248, Fat: 15.9g, Carbohydrates: 6.5g, Sugar: 3.3g, Protein: 20.4g, Sodium: 155mg

10. Peanut Butter Banana Bread

Preparation Time: 15 minutes

Cooking time: 40 minutes

Servings: 6

Ingredients:

1 cup plus 1 tablespoon all-purpose flour

1¼ teaspoons baking powder

1 large egg

2 medium ripe bananas, peeled and mashed

¾ cup walnuts, roughly chopped

¼ teaspoon salt

1/3 cup granulated sugar

¼ cup canola oil

2 tablespoons creamy peanut butter

2 tablespoons sour cream

1 teaspoon vanilla extract

Directions:

Preheat the Air fryer to 330 o F and grease a non-stick baking dish.

Mix together the flour, baking powder and salt in a bowl.

Whisk together egg with sugar, canola oil, sour cream, peanut butter and vanilla extract in a bowl.

Stir in the bananas and beat until well combined.

Now, add the flour mixture and fold in the walnuts gently.

Mix until combined and transfer the mixture evenly into the prepared baking dish.

Arrange the baking dish in an Air fryer basket and cook for about 40 minutes.

Remove from the Air fryer and place onto a wire rack to cool.

Cut the bread into desired size slices and serve.

Nutrition:

Calories: 384, Fat: 2.6g, Carbohydrates: 39.3g, Sugar: 16.6g, Protein: 8.9g, Sodium: 189mg

11. Yummy Savory French Toasts

Preparation Time: 10 minutes

Cooking time: 4 minutes

Servings: 2

Ingredients:

¼ cup chickpea flour
3 tablespoons onion, chopped finely
2 teaspoons green chili, seeded and chopped finely
Water, as required
4 bread slices
½ teaspoon red chili powder
¼ teaspoon ground turmeric
¼ teaspoon ground cumin
Salt, to taste

Directions:
Preheat the Air fryer to 375 o F and line an Air fryer pan with a foil paper. Mix together all the ingredients in a large bowl except the bread slices. Spread the mixture over both sides of the bread slices and transfer into the Air fryer pan. Cook for about 4 minutes and remove from the Air fryer to serve.

Nutrition:
Calories: 151, Fat: 2.3g, Carbohydrates: 26.7g, Sugar: 4.3g, Protein: 6.5g, Sodium: 234mg

12. Aromatic Potato Hash

Preparation Time: 10 minutes
Cooking time: 42 minutes
Servings: 4
Ingredients:
2 teaspoons butter, melted
1 medium onion, chopped
½ of green bell pepper, seeded and chopped
1½ pound russet potatoes, peeled and cubed
5 eggs, beaten
½ teaspoon dried thyme, crushed
½ teaspoon dried savory, crushed
Salt and black pepper, to taste
Directions:
Preheat the Air fryer to 390 o F and grease an Air fryer pan with melted butter.
Put onion and bell pepper in the Air fryer pan and cook for about 5 minutes.
Add the potatoes, thyme, savory, salt and black pepper and cook for about 30 minutes.
Meanwhile, heat a greased skillet on medium heat and stir in the beaten eggs.
Cook for about 1 minute on each side and remove from the skillet.
Cut it into small pieces and transfer the egg pieces into the Air fryer pan.
Cook for about 5 more minutes and serve warm.
Nutrition:
Calories: 229, Fat: 7.6g, Carbohydrates: 30.8g, Sugar: 4.2g, Protein: 10.3g, Sodium: 103mg

13. Pumpkin and Yogurt Bread

Preparation Time: 10 minutes

Cooking time: 15 minutes
Servings: 4
Ingredients:
2 large eggs
8 tablespoons pumpkin puree
6 tablespoons banana flour
4 tablespoons plain Greek yogurt
6 tablespoons oats
4 tablespoons honey
2 tablespoons vanilla essence
Pinch of ground nutmeg
Directions:
Preheat the Air fryer to 360 o F and grease a loaf pan.
Mix together all the ingredients except oats in a bowl and beat with the hand mixer until smooth.
Add oats and mix until well combined.
Transfer the mixture into the prepared loaf pan and place in the Air fryer.
Cook for about 15 minutes and remove from the Air fryer.
Place onto a wire rack to cool and cut the bread into desired size slices to serve.
Nutrition:
Calories: 212, Fat: 3.4g, Carbohydrates: 36g, Sugar: 20.5g, Protein: 6.6g, Sodium: 49mg

14. Zucchini Fritters

Preparation Time: 15 minutes
Cooking time: 7 minutes
Servings: 4
Ingredients:
10½ ounces zucchini, grated and squeezed
7 ounces Halloumi cheese
¼ cup all-purpose flour
2 eggs
1 teaspoon fresh dill, minced
Salt and black pepper, to taste
Directions:
Preheat the Air fryer to 360 o F and grease a baking dish.
Mix together all the ingredients in a large bowl.
Make small fritters from this mixture and place them on the prepared baking dish.
Transfer the dish in the Air Fryer basket and cook for about 7 minutes.
Dish out and serve warm.
Nutrition:
Calories: 250, Fat: 17.2g, Carbohydrates: 10g, Sugar: 2.7g, Protein: 15.2g, Sodium: 330mg

15. Chicken Omelet

Preparation Time: 15 minutes
Cooking time: 16 minutes
Servings: 8

Ingredients:
1 teaspoon butter
1 onion, chopped
½ jalapeño pepper, seeded and chopped
3 eggs
¼ cup chicken, cooked and shredded
Salt and black pepper, to taste
Directions:
Preheat the Air fryer to 355 o F and grease an Air Fryer pan.
Heat butter in a frying pan over medium heat and add onions.
Sauté for about 5 minutes and add jalapeño pepper.
Sauté for about 1 minute and stir in the chicken.
Remove from the heat and keep aside.
Meanwhile, whisk together the eggs, salt, and black pepper in a bowl.
Place the chicken mixture into the prepared pan and top with the egg mixture.
Cook for about 10 minutes until completely done and serve hot.
Nutrition:
Calories: 161, Fat: 3.4g, Carbohydrates: 5.9g, Sugar: 3g, Protein: 14.1g, Sodium:
197mg
Breakfast Egg Bowls Preparation time: 10 minutes
Cooking time: 20 minutes
Servings: 4
Ingredients:
4 dinner rolls, tops cut off and insides scooped out
4 tablespoons heavy cream
4 eggs
4 tablespoons mixed chives and parsley
Salt and black pepper to the taste
4 tablespoons parmesan, grated
Directions:
Arrange dinner rolls on a baking sheet and crack an egg in each.
Divide heavy cream, mixed herbs in each roll and season with salt and pepper.
Sprinkle parmesan on top of your rolls, place them in your air fryer and cook at
350 degrees F for 20 minutes.
Divide your bread bowls on plates and serve for breakfast.
Enjoy!Nutrition: calories 238, fat 4, fiber 7, carbs 14, protein 7Delicious Breakfast
Soufflé Preparation time: 10 minutes
Cooking time: 8 minutes
Servings: 4Ingredients:
4 eggs, whisk
4 tablespoons heavy cream
A pinch of crushed red pepper
2 tablespoons parsley, chopped
2 tablespoons chives, minced
Salt and black pepper taste to taste
Directions:

In a cup, combine the eggs with the oil, the vinegar, the heavy cream, the chili pepper, the parsley and the chives, mix well and split into 4 soufflé bowls. Organize the dishes in the air fryer and boil the soufflés at 350 degrees F to 8 minutes.

Serve when hot, Enjoy!Nutrition: calories 300, fat 7, fiber 9, carbs 15, protein 6Air Fried Sandwich Preparation time: 10 minutes

Cooking time: 6 minutes

Servings: 2

Ingredients:

2 English muffins, halved

2 eggs

2 bacon strips

Salt and black pepper to the tasteDirections:

Crack eggs in your air fryer, add bacon on top, cover and cook at 392 degrees F for 6 minutes.

Heat up your English muffin halves in your microwave for a few seconds, divide eggs on 2 halves, add bacon on top, season with salt and pepper, cover with the other 2 English muffins and serve for breakfast.

Enjoy!Nutrition: calories 261, fat 5, fiber 8, carbs 12, protein 4

16. Rustic Breakfast

Preparation time: 10 minutes

Cooking time: 13 minutes

Servings: 4Ingredients:

7 ounces baby spinach

8 chestnuts mushrooms, halved

8 tomatoes, halved

1 garlic clove, minced

4 chipolatas

4 bacon slices, chopped

Salt and black pepper to the taste

4 eggs

Cooking sprayDirections:

Grease a cooking pan with the oil and add tomatoes, garlic and mushrooms.

Add bacon and chipolatas, also add spinach and crack eggs at the end.

Season with salt and pepper, place pan in the cooking basket of your air fryer and cook for 13 minutes at 350 degrees F.

Divide among plates and serve for breakfast.

Enjoy!Nutrition: calories 312, fat 6, fiber 8, carbs 15, protein 5

17. Egg Muffins

Preparation time: 10 minutes

Cooking time: 15 minutes

Servings: 4Ingredients:

1 egg

2 tablespoons olive oil

3 tablespoons milk

3.5 ounces white flour

1 tablespoon baking powder

2 ounces parmesan, grated

A splash of Worcestershire sauceDirections:

In a bowl, mix egg with flour, oil, baking powder, milk, Worcestershire and parmesan, whisk well and divide into 4 silicon muffin cups.

Arrange cups in your air fryer's cooking basket, cover and cook at 392, degrees F for 15 minutes.

Serve warm for breakfast.

Enjoy!Nutrition: calories 251, fat 6, fiber 8, carbs 9, protein 3

Lunch Recipes
18. Yogurt Garlic Chicken

Preparation Time: 30 min

Cooking time: 60 min

Servings: 6

Ingredients:

Pita bread rounds, halved (6 pieces)

English cucumber, sliced thinly, w/ each slice halved (1 cup)

Olive oil (3 tablespoons)

Black pepper, freshly ground (1/2 teaspoon)

Chicken thighs, skinless, boneless (20 ounces)

Bell pepper, red, sliced into half-inch portions (1 piece)

Garlic cloves, chopped finely (4 pieces)

Cumin, ground (1/2 teaspoon)

Red onion, medium, sliced into half-inch wedges (1 piece)

Yogurt, plain, fat free (1/2 cup)

Lemon juice (2 tablespoons)

Salt (1 ½ teaspoons)

Red pepper flakes, crushed (1/2 teaspoon)

Allspice, ground (1/2 teaspoon)

Bell pepper, yellow, sliced into half-inch portions (1 piece)

Yogurt sauce

Olive oil (2 tablespoons)

Salt (1/4 teaspoon)

Parsley, flat leaf, chopped finely (1 tablespoon)

Yogurt, plain, fat free (1 cup)

Lemon juice, fresh (1 tablespoon)

Garlic clove, chopped finely (1 piece)

Directions:

Mix the yogurt (1/2 cup), garlic cloves (4 pieces), olive oil (1 tablespoon), salt (1 teaspoon), lemon juice (2 tablespoons), pepper (1/4 teaspoon), allspice, cumin, and pepper flakes. Stir in the chicken and coat well. Cover and marinate in the fridge for two hours.

Preheat the air fryer at 400 degrees Fahrenheit.

Grease a rimmed baking sheet (18x13-inch) with cooking spray.

Toss the bell peppers and onion with remaining olive oil (2 tablespoons), pepper (1/4 teaspoon), and salt (1/2 teaspoon).

Arrange veggies on the baking sheet's left side and the marinated chicken thighs (drain first) on the right side. Cook in the air fryer for twenty-five to thirty minutes.

Mix the yogurt sauce ingredients.

Slice air-fried chicken into half-inch strips.

Top each pita round with chicken strips, roasted veggies, cucumbers, and yogurt sauce.

Nutrition: Calories 380 Fat 15.0 g Protein 26.0 g Carbohydrates 34.0 g

19. Lemony Parmesan Salmon

Preparation Time: 10 min
Cooking time: 25 min
Servings: 4
Ingredients:
Butter, melted (2 tablespoons)
Green onions, sliced thinly (2 tablespoons)
Breadcrumbs, white, fresh (3/4 cup)
Thyme leaves, dried (1/4 teaspoon)
Salmon fillet, 1 ¼-pound (1 piece)
Salt (1/4 teaspoon)
Parmesan cheese, grated (1/4 cup)
Lemon peel, grated (2 teaspoons)
Directions:
Preheat the air fryer at 350 degrees Fahrenheit.
Mist cooking spray onto a baking pan (shallow). Fill with pat-dried salmon. Brush salmon with butter (1 tablespoon) before sprinkling with salt.
Combine the breadcrumbs with onions, thyme, lemon peel, cheese, and remaining butter (1 tablespoon).
Cover salmon with the breadcrumb mixture. Air-fry for fifteen to twenty-five minutes.
Nutrition: Calories 290 Fat 16.0 g Protein 33.0 g Carbohydrates 4.0 g

20. Easiest Tuna Cobbler Ever

Preparation time: 15 min Cooking time: 25 min
Servings: 4
Ingredients:
Water, cold (1/3 cup)
Tuna, canned, drained (10 ounces)
Sweet pickle relish (2 tablespoons)
Mixed vegetables, frozen (1 ½ cups)
Soup, cream of chicken, condensed (10 ¾ ounces)
Pimientos, sliced, drained (2 ounces)
Lemon juice (1 teaspoon)
Paprika
Directions:
Preheat the air fryer at 375 degrees Fahrenheit.
Mist cooking spray into a round casserole (1 ½ quarts).
Mix the frozen vegetables with milk, soup, lemon juice, relish, pimientos, and tuna in a saucepan. Cook for six to eight minutes over medium heat.
Fill the casserole with the tuna mixture.
Mix the biscuit mix with cold water to form a soft dough. Beat for half a minute before dropping by four spoonfuls into the casserole.
Dust the dish with paprika before air-frying for twenty to twenty-five minutes.
Nutrition: Calories 320 Fat 11.0 g Protein 28.0 g Carbohydrates 31.0 g

21. Deliciously Homemade Pork Buns

Preparation time: 20 min
Cooking time: 25 min
Servings: 8

Ingredients:

Green onions, sliced thinly (3 pieces)

Egg, beaten (1 piece)

Pulled pork, diced, w/ barbecue sauce (1 cup)

Buttermilk biscuits, refrigerated (16 1/3 ounces)

Soy sauce (1 teaspoon)

Directions:

Preheat the air fryer at 325 degrees Fahrenheit.

Use parchment paper to line your baking sheet.

Combine pork with green onions.

Separate and press the dough to form 8 four-inch rounds.

Fill each biscuit round's center with two tablespoons of pork mixture. Cover with the dough edges and seal by pinching. Arrange the buns on the sheet and brush with a mixture of soy sauce and egg.

Cook in the air fryer for twenty to twenty-five minutes.

Nutrition: Calories 240 Fat 9.0 g Protein 8.0 g Carbohydrates 29.0 g

22. Mouthwatering Tuna Melts

Preparation time: 15 min

Cooking time: 20 min

Servings: 8

Ingredients:

Salt (1/8 teaspoon)

Onion, chopped (1/3 cup)

Biscuits, refrigerated, flaky layers (16 1/3 ounces)

Tuna, water packed, drained (10 ounces)

Mayonnaise (1/3 cup)

Pepper (1/8 teaspoon)

Cheddar cheese, shredded (4 ounces)

Tomato, chopped

Sour cream

Lettuce, shredded

Directions:

Preheat the air fryer at 325 degrees Fahrenheit.

Mist cooking spray onto a cookie sheet.

Mix tuna with mayonnaise, pepper, salt, and onion.

Separate dough so you have 8 biscuits; press each into 5-inch rounds.

Arrange 4 biscuit rounds on the sheet. Fill at the center with tuna mixture before topping with cheese. Cover with the remaining biscuit rounds and press to seal. Air-fry for fifteen to twenty minutes. Slice each sandwich into halves. Serve each piece topped with lettuce, tomato, and sour cream.

23. Nutrition: Calories 320 Fat 18.0 g Protein 14.0 g Carbohydrates 27.0 g Bacon Wings

Preparation time: 15 min

Cooking time: 1 hr 15 min

Servings: 12

Ingredients:

Bacon strips (12 pieces)
Paprika (1 teaspoon)
Black pepper (1 tablespoon)
Oregano (1 teaspoon)
Chicken wings (12 pieces)
Kosher salt (1 tablespoon)
Brown sugar (1 tablespoon)
Chili powder (1 teaspoon)
Celery sticks
Blue cheese dressing
Directions:
Preheat the air fryer at 325 degrees Fahrenheit.
Mix sugar, salt, chili powder, oregano, pepper, and paprika. Coat chicken wings with this dry rub.
Wrap a bacon strip around each wing. Arrange wrapped wings in the air fryer basket.
Cook for thirty minutes on each side in the air fryer. Let cool for five minutes. Serve and enjoy with celery and blue cheese.
Nutrition: Calories 100 Fat 5.0 g Protein 10.0 g Carbohydrates 2.0 g

24. Pepper Pesto Lamb

Preparation time: 15 min
Cooking time: 1 hr 15 min
Servings: 12
Ingredients:
Pesto
Rosemary leaves, fresh (1/4 cup)
Garlic cloves (3 pieces)
Parsley, fresh, packed firmly (3/4 cup)
Mint leaves, fresh (1/4 cup)
Olive oil (2 tablespoons)
Lamb
Red bell peppers, roasted, drained (7 ½ ounces)
Leg of lamb, boneless, rolled (5 pounds)
Seasoning, lemon pepper (2 teaspoons)
Directions:
Preheat the oven at 325 degrees Fahrenheit.
Mix the pesto ingredients in the food processor.
Unroll the lamb and cover the cut side with pesto. Top with roasted peppers before rolling up the lamb and tying with kitchen twine.
Coat lamb with seasoning (lemon pepper) and air-fry for one hour.
Nutrition: Calories 310 Fat 15.0 g Protein 40.0 g Carbohydrates 1.0 g

25. Tuna Spinach Casserole

Preparation time: 30 min
Cooking time: 25 min
Servings: 8
Ingredients:
Mushroom soup, creamy (18 ounces)

Milk (1/2 cup)

White tuna, solid, in-water, drained (12 ounces)

Crescent dinner rolls, refrigerated (8 ounces)

Egg noodles, wide, uncooked (8 ounces)

Cheddar cheese, shredded (8 ounces)

Spinach, chopped, frozen, thawed, drained (9 ounces)

Lemon peel grated (2 teaspoons)

Directions:

Preheat the oven at 350 degrees Fahrenheit.

Mist cooking spray onto a glass baking dish (11x7-inch).

Follow package directions in cooking and draining the noodles.

Stir the cheese (1 ½ cups) and soup together in a skillet heated on medium. Once cheese melts, stir in your noodles, milk, spinach, tuna, and lemon peel. Once bubbling, pour into the prepped dish.

Unroll the dough and sprinkle with remaining cheese (1/2 cup). Roll up dough and pinch at the seams to seal. Slice into 8 portions and place over the tuna mixture.

Air-fry for twenty to twenty-five minutes.

Nutrition: Calories 400 Fat 19.0 g Protein 21.0 g Carbohydrates 35.0 g

26. Greek Style Mini Burger Pies

Preparation time: 15 min

Cooking time: 40 min

Servings: 6

Ingredients:

Burger mixture:

Onion, large, chopped (1 piece)

Red bell peppers, roasted, diced (1/2 cup)

Ground lamb, 80% lean (1 pound)

Red pepper flakes (1/4 teaspoon)

Feta cheese, crumbled (2 ounces)

Baking mixture

Milk (1/2 cup)

Biscuit mix, classic (1/2 cup)

Eggs (2 pieces)

Directions:

Preheat the air fryer at 350 degrees Fahrenheit.

Grease 12 muffin cups using cooking spray.

Cook the onion and beef in a skillet heated on medium-high. Once beef is browned and cooked through, drain and let cool for five minutes. Stir together with feta cheese, roasted red peppers, and red pepper flakes.

Whisk the baking mixture ingredients together. Fill each muffin cup with baking mixture (1 tablespoon).

Air-fry for twenty-five to thirty minutes. Let cool before serving.

Nutrition: Calories 270 Fat 15.0 g Protein 19.0 g Carbohydrates 13.0 g

27. Family Fun Pizza

Preparation time: 30 min

Cooking time: 25 min

Servings: 16
Ingredients:
Pizza crust
Water, warm (1 cup)
Salt (1/2 teaspoon)
Flour, whole wheat (1 cup)
Olive oil (2 tablespoons)
Dry yeast, quick active (1 package)
Flour, all purpose (1 ½ cups)
Cornmeal
Olive oil
Filling:
Onion, chopped (1 cup)
Mushrooms, sliced, drained (4 ounces)
Garlic cloves, chopped finely (2 pieces)
Parmesan cheese, grated (1/4 cup)
Ground lamb, 80% lean (1 pound)
Italian seasoning (1 teaspoon)
Pizza sauce (8 ounces)
Mozzarella cheese, shredded (2 cups)
Directions:
Mix yeast with warm water. Combine with flours, oil (2 tablespoons), and salt by stirring and then beating vigorously for half a minute. Let the dough sit for twenty minutes.
Preheat the air fryer at 350 degrees Fahrenheit.
Prep 2 square pans (8-inch) by greasing with oil before sprinkling with cornmeal. Cut the rested dough in half; place each half inside each pan. Set aside, covered, for thirty to forty-five minutes. Cook in the air fryer for twenty to twenty-two minutes.
Sauté the onion, beef, garlic, and Italian seasoning until beef is completely cooked. Drain and set aside.
Cover the air-fried crusts with pizza sauce before topping with beef mixture, cheeses, and mushrooms.
Return to the air fryer and cook for twenty minutes.
Nutrition: Calories 215 Fat 10.0 g Protein 13.0 g Carbohydrates 20.0 g

28. Tso's Cauliflower

Preparation Time: 5 minutes
Cooking Time: 25 minutes
Servings: 2
Ingredients:
1 head cauliflower, cut in florets
¾ cup all-purpose flour, divided
3 eggs
1 cup panko breadcrumbs
Tso sauce
Canola or peanut oil
2 tbsp oyster sauce

¼ cup soy sauce

2 tsp chili paste

2 tbsp rice wine vinegar

2 tbsp sugar

¼ cup water

Directions:

Add cauliflower to a large bowl and sprinkle ¼ cup flour over it.

Whisk eggs in one bowl, spread panko crumbs in another, and put remaining flour in a third bowl.

Dredge the cauliflower florets through the flour then dip in the eggs.

Coat them with breadcrumbs.

Place the coated cauliflower florets in the air fryer basket and spray them with cooking oil.

Return the fryer basket to the air fryer and cook on air fry mode for 15 minutes at 400 degrees F.

Prepare the Tso sauce by mixing all its ingredients in a saucepan.

Stir and cook this mixture for 10 minutes until it thickens.

Pour this sauce over the air fried cauliflower florets.

Enjoy.

Nutrition:

Calories 301

Total Fat 12.2 g

Saturated Fat 2.4 g

Cholesterol 110 mg

Sodium 276 mg

Total Carbs 12.5 g

Fiber 0.9 g

Sugar 1.4 g

Protein 8.8 g

29. Crispy Hot Sauce Chicken

Preparation Time: 5 minutes

Cooking Time: 30 minutes

Total Time: 35 minutes

Servings: 4

Ingredients:

2 cups buttermilk

1 tbsp hot sauce

1 whole chicken, cut up

1 cup Kentucky Kernel flour

Oil for spraying

Directions:

Whisk hot sauce with buttermilk in a large bowl.

Add chicken pieces to the buttermilk mixture and marinate for 1 hour in the refrigerator.

Dredge the chicken through seasoned flour and shake off the excess.

Place the coated chicken in the air fryer basket and spray them with cooking oil.

Return the fryer basket to the air fryer and cook on air fry mode for 30 minutes at 380 degrees F.

Flip the chicken pieces once cooked half way through.

Enjoy right away.

Nutrition:

Calories 695

Total Fat 17.5 g

Saturated Fat 4.8 g

Cholesterol 283 mg

Sodium 355 mg

Total Carbs 6.4 g

Fiber 1.8 g

Sugar 0.8 g

Protein 117.4 g

30. Teriyaki Chicken Meatballs

Preparation Time: 5 minutes

Cooking Time: 10 minutes

Total Time: 15 minutes

Servings: 4

Ingredients:

For Chicken Meatballs

1 lb ground chicken

½ cup gluten-free oat flour

1 small onion, chopped

¾ tsp garlic powder

¾ tsp crushed chili flakes

1 tsp dried cilantro leaves

Salt, to taste

Scallions, for garnish

Sesame seeds, for garnish

For Spicy Teriyaki Sauce

¼ cup sweet and sour sauce

2 tbsp rice vinegar

2 tbsp soy sauce (light)

2 tbsp honey

½ tsp hot sauce (optional)

1 tsp crushed chili flakes

¾ tsp garlic powder

¾ tsp ginger powder

Directions:

Add the ingredients for the meatballs in a suitable bowl.

Mix well and knead the dough.

Make small meatballs out of this dough and place them in the air fryer basket.

Spray them with cooking oil.

Return the fryer basket to the air fryer and cook on air fry mode for 10 minutes at 350 degrees F.

Meanwhile, mix all the ingredients for the teriyaki sauce in a saucepan.

Stir and cook this sauce until it thickens,
Add the air fried balls to the sauce.
Garnish with scallions and sesame seeds.
Enjoy.
Nutrition:
Calories 401
Total Fat 8.9 g
Saturated Fat 4.5 g
Cholesterol 57 mg
Sodium 340 mg
Total Carbs 24.7 g
Fiber 1.2 g
Sugar 1.3 g
Protein 55.3 g

31. Orange Tofu

Preparation Time: 5 minutes
Cooking Time: 20 minutes
Total Time: 25 minutes
Servings: 2
Ingredients:
1 lb extra-firm tofu, drained and pressed
1 tbsp tamari
1 tbsp cornstarch
For Sauce:
1 tsp orange zest
1/3 cup orange juice
½ cup water
2 tsp cornstarch
¼ tsp crushed red pepper flakes
1 tsp fresh ginger, minced
1 tsp fresh garlic, minced
1 tbsp pure maple syrup
How to Prepare:
Dice the squeezed tofu into cubes then place them in a Ziploc bag.
Add tamari and 1 tablespoon of cornstarch to the tofu.
Seal the tofu bag and shake well to coat.
Spread this tofu in the air fryer basket and spray them with cooking oil.
Return the fryer basket to the air fryer and cook on air fry mode for 15 minutes at 350 degrees F.
Air fry the tofu cubes in two batches.
Mix all the ingredients for the sauce in a saucepan and stir cook until it thickens.
Toss in fried tofu and mix well.
Enjoy.
Nutrition:
Calories 427
Total Fat 31.1 g
Saturated Fat 4.2 g

Cholesterol 123 mg
Sodium 86 mg
Total Carbs 9 g
Sugar 12.4 g
Fiber 19.8 g
Protein 23.5 g

32. Madagascan Stew

Preparation Time: 5 minutes
Cooking Time: 19 minutes
Total Time: 24 minutes
Servings: 4

Ingredients:
7 oz baby new potatoes
1 tbsp oil
½ onion, finely diced
1 ¼ cups canned black beans, drained
1 ¼ cups canned kidney beans, drained
3 cloves garlic, minced
1 tbsp pureed ginger
2 large tomatoes, chopped
1 tbsp tomato puree
Salt
Black pepper
1 cup vegetable stock
½ tbsp cornstarch
1 tbsp water
1 large handful arugula
Cooked rice, to serve (optional)
Directions:
Cut the potatoes into quarters and toss them with cooking oil.
Place the potatoes in the air fryer basket.
Add onion to the basket and continue air frying for another 4 minutes.
Transfer them to a saucepan and place over medium heat.
Add garlic, ginger, beans, tomatoes, seasoning, vegetable stock, and tomato puree.
Mix cornstarch with water in a bowl and pour into the pan.
Simmer this mixture for 15 minutes.
Add arugula and cook for another 4 minutes.
Serve with rice.
Nutrition:
Calories 398
Total Fat 13.8 g
Saturated Fat 5.1 g
Cholesterol 200 mg
Sodium 272 mg
Total Carbs 53.6 g

Fiber 1 g
Sugar 1.3 g
Protein 11.8 g

33. Tofu Sushi Burrito

Preparation Time: 5 minutes
Cooking Time: 15 minutes
Total Time: 20 minutes
Servings: 2
Ingredients:
¼ block extra firm tofu, pressed and sliced
1 tbsp low-sodium soy sauce
¼ tsp ground ginger
¼ tsp garlic powder
Sriracha sauce, to taste
2 cups cooked sushi rice
2 sheets nori
Filling:
¼ avocado, sliced
3 tbsp mango, sliced
1 green onion, finely chopped
2 tbsp pickled ginger
2 tbsp panko breadcrumbs
Directions:
Whisk ginger, garlic, soy sauce, sriracha sauce, and tofu in a large bowl.
Let them marinate for 10 minutes then transfer them to the air fryer basket.
Return the fryer basket to the air fryer and cook on air fry mode for 15 minutes at 370 degrees F.
Toss the tofu cubes after 8 minutes then resume cooking.
Spread a nori sheet on a work surface and top it with a layer of sushi rice.
Place tofu and half of the other filling ingredients over the rice.
Roll the sheet tightly to secure the filling inside.
Repeat the same steps to make another sushi roll.
Enjoy.
Nutrition:
Calories 372
Total Fat 11.8 g
Saturated Fat 4.4 g
Cholesterol 62 mg
Sodium 871 mg
Total Carbs 45.8 g
Fiber 0.6 g
Sugar 27.3 g
Protein 34 g

34. Rosemary Brussels Sprouts

Preparation Time: 5 minutes
Cooking Time: 13 minutes
Total Time: 18 minutes

Servings: 2
Ingredients:
3 tbsp olive oil
2 garlic cloves, minced
½ tsp salt
¼ tsp pepper
1 lb Brussels sprouts, trimmed and halved
½ cup panko breadcrumbs
1 ½ tsp fresh rosemary, minced
Directions:
Let your air fryer preheat at 350 degrees F.
Mix oil, garlic, salt, and pepper in a bowl and heat for 30 seconds in the microwave.
Add 2 tablespoons of this mixture to the Brussel sprouts in a bowl and mix well to coat.
Spread the sprouts in the air fryer basket.
Return the fryer basket to the air fryer and cook on air fry mode for 5 minutes at 220 degrees F.
Toss the sprouts well and continue air frying for 8 minutes more.
Mix the remaining oil mixture with rosemary and breadcrumbs in a bowl.
Spread this mixture over the Brussel sprouts and return the basket to the fryer.
Air fry them for 5 minutes.
Enjoy.
Nutrition:
Calories 246
Total Fat 7.4 g
Saturated Fat 4.6 g
Cholesterol 105 mg
Sodium 353 mg
Total Carbs 9.4 g
Sugar 6.5 g
Fiber 2.7 g
Protein 37.2 g

35. Peach-Bourbon Wings

Preparation Time: 5 minutes
Cooking Time: 14 minutes
Total Time: 19 minutes
Servings: 8
Ingredients:
½ cup peach preserves
1 tbsp brown sugar
1 garlic cloves, minced
¼ tsp salt
2 tbsp white vinegar
2 tbsp bourbon
1 tsp cornstarch
1½ tsp water

2 lbs chicken wings

Directions:

Let your air fryer preheat at 400 degrees F.

Add salt, garlic, and brown sugar to a food processor and blend well until smooth.

Transfer this mixture to a saucepan and add bourbon, peach preserves, and vinegar.

Stir cook this mixture to a boil then reduce heat to a simmer.

Cook for 6 minutes until the mixture thickens.

Mix cornstarch with water and pour this mixture in the saucepan.

Stir cook for 2 minutes until it thickens. Keep ¼ cup of this sauce aside.

Place the wings in the air fryer basket and brush them with prepared sauce.

Return the fryer basket to the air fryer and cook on air fry mode for 6 minutes at 350 degrees F.

Flip the wings and brush them again with the sauce.

Air fry the wings for another 8 minutes.

Serve with reserved sauce.

Nutrition:

Calories 293

Total Fat 16 g

Saturated Fat 2.3 g

Cholesterol 75 mg

Sodium 386 mg

Total Carbs 5.2 g

Sugar 2.6 g

Fiber 1.9 g

Protein 34.2 g

36. Reuben Calzones

Preparation Time: 5 minutes

Cooking Time: 12 minutes

Total Time: 17 minutes

Servings: 4

Ingredients:

1 tube (13.8 ounces) refrigerated pizza crust

4 slices Swiss cheese

1 cup sauerkraut, rinsed and well drained

½ lb corned beef, sliced & cooked

Directions:

Let your air fryer preheat at 400 degrees F. Grease the air fryer basket with cooking oil.

Spread the pizza crust on a lightly floured surface into a 12-inch square.

Slice the crust into four smaller squares.

Place one slice of cheese, ¼ of the sauerkraut, and 1 slice corned beef over each square diagonally.

Fold the squares in half diagonally to form a triangle and pinch the edges together.

Place 2 triangles in the air fryer basket at a time and spray them with cooking oil.

Return the fryer basket to the air fryer and cook on air fry mode for 12 minutes at 350 degrees F.

Air fry the remaining calazone triangles.

Enjoy with fresh salad.

Nutrition:

Calories 604

Total Fat 30.6 g

Saturated Fat 13.1 g

Cholesterol 131 mg

Sodium 834 mg

Total Carbs 31.4 g

Fiber 0.2 g

Sugar 20.3 g

Protein 54.6 g

37. Mushroom Maple Rice

Preparation Time: 5 minutes

Cooking Time: 15 minutes

Total Time: 20 minutes

Servings: 4

Ingredients:

16 oz jasmine rice, cooked

½ cup soy sauce

4 tbsp maple syrup

4 cloves garlic, finely chopped

2 tsp Chinese five spice

½ tsp ground ginger

4 tbsp white wine

16 oz cremini mushrooms, cut in half

½ cup frozen peas

Directions:

Mix soy sauce with maple syrup, garlic, Chinese five spice, ginger, and white wine in a bowl.

Spread the mushrooms in the air fryer basket and spray them with cooking oil.

Return the fryer basket to the air fryer and cook on air fry mode for 10 minutes at 350 degrees F.

Add peas and prepared sauce over the mushrooms and mix well.

Return the fryer basket to the air fryer and cook on air fry mode for 5 minutes at 350 degrees F.

Mix the mushrooms with the rice in a pot.

Enjoy.

Nutrition:

Calories 311

Total Fat 25.5 g

Saturated Fat 12.4 g

Cholesterol 69 mg

Sodium 58 mg

Total Carbs 32.4 g

Fiber 0.7 g
Sugar 0.3 g
Protein 18.4 g

Poultry Recipes

Creamy Coconut Chicken Preparation time: 2 hours

Cooking time: 25 minutes

Servings: 4Ingredients:

4 big chicken legs

5 teaspoons turmeric powder

2 tablespoons ginger, grated

Salt and black pepper to the taste

4 tablespoons coconut creamDirections:

In a bowl, mix cream with turmeric, ginger, salt and pepper, whisk, add chicken pieces, toss them well and leave aside for 2 hours.

Transfer chicken to your preheated air fryer, cook at 370 degrees F for 25 minutes, divide among plates and serve with a side salad.

Enjoy!Nutrition: calories 300, fat 4, fiber 12, carbs 22, protein 20

 Chinese Chicken Wings Preparation time: 2 hours

Cooking time: 15 minutes

Servings: 6Ingredients:

16 chicken wings

2 tablespoons honey

2 tablespoons soy sauce

Salt and black pepper to the taste

¼ teaspoon white pepper

3 tablespoons lime juiceDirections:

In a bowl, mix honey with soy sauce, salt, black and white pepper and lime juice, whisk well, add chicken pieces, toss to coat and keep in the fridge for 2 hours.

Transfer chicken to your air fryer, cook at 370 degrees F for 6 minutes on each side, increase heat to 400 degrees F and cook for 3 minutes more.

Serve hot.

Enjoy!Nutrition: calories 372, fat 9, fiber 10, carbs 37, protein 24

Herbed Chicken Preparation time: 30 minutes

Cooking time: 40 minutes

Servings: 4Ingredients:

1 whole chicken

Salt and black pepper to the taste

1 teaspoon garlic powder

1 teaspoon onion powder

½ teaspoon thyme, dried

1 teaspoon rosemary, dried

1 tablespoon lemon juice

2 tablespoons olive oilDirections:

Use pepper and salt to season the chicken, mix with thyme, rosemary, garlic powder and onion powder, rub with lemon juice and olive oil and leave aside for 30 minutes.

Put chicken in your air fryer and cook at 360 degrees F for 20 minutes on each side.

Leave chicken aside to cool down, carve and serve.

Enjoy!Nutrition: calories 390, fat 10, fiber 5, carbs 22, protein 20 Chicken Parmesan Preparation time: 10 minutes

Cooking time: 15 minutes

Servings: 4Ingredients:

2 cups panko bread crumbs

¼ cup parmesan, grated

½ teaspoon garlic powder

2 cups white flour

1 egg, whisked

1 and ½ pounds chicken cutlets, skinless and boneless

Salt and black pepper to the taste

1 cup mozzarella, grated

2 cups tomato sauce

3 tablespoons basil, choppedDirections:

In a bowl, mix panko with parmesan and garlic powder and stir.

Put flour in a second bowl and the egg in a third.

Season chicken with salt and pepper, dip in flour, then in egg mix and in panko.

Put chicken pieces in your air fryer and cook them at 360 degrees F for 3 minutes on each side.

Transfer chicken to a baking dish that fits your air fryer, add tomato sauce and top with mozzarella, introduce in your air fryer and cook at 375 degrees F for 7 minutes.

Divide among plates, sprinkle basil on top and serve.

Enjoy!Nutrition: calories 304, fat 12, fiber 11, carbs 22, protein 15

 Mexican Chicken Preparation time: 10 minutes

Cooking time: 20 minutes

Servings: 4Ingredients:

16 ounces salsa verde

1 tablespoon olive oil

Salt and black pepper to the taste

1 pound chicken breast, boneless and skinless

1 and ½ cup Monterey Jack cheese, grated

¼ cup cilantro, chopped

1 teaspoon garlic powder

Directions:

Pour salsa verde in a baking dish that fits your air fryer, season chicken with salt, pepper, garlic powder, brush with olive oil and place it over your salsa verde.

put in your air fryer and boil at 380 degrees F for 20 minutes.

Sprinkle cheese on top and cook for 2 minutes more.

Divide among plates and serve hot.

Enjoy!Nutrition: calories 340, fat 18, fiber 14, carbs 32, protein 18

 Creamy Chicken, Rice and Peas Preparation time: 10 minutes

Cooking time: 30 minutes

Servings: 4Ingredients:

1 pound chicken breasts, skinless, boneless and cut into quarters

1 cup white rice, already cooked

Salt and black pepper to the taste

1 tablespoon olive oil

3 garlic cloves, minced

1 yellow onion, chopped

½ cup white wine

¼ cup heavy cream

1 cup chicken stock

¼ cup parsley, chopped

2 cups peas, frozen

1 and ½ cups parmesan, gratedDirections:

Season chicken breasts with salt and pepper, drizzle half of the oil over them, rub well, put in your air fryer's basket and cook them at 360 degrees F for 6 minutes. Warm the pot with the remaining oil over medium high heat, add garlic, onion, wine, stock, salt, pepper and heavy cream, stir, bring to a simmer and cook for 9 minutes.

Transfer chicken breasts to a heat proof dish that fits your air fryer, add peas, rice and cream mix over them, toss, sprinkle parmesan and parsley all over, place in your air fryer and cook at 420 degrees F for 10 minutes.

Divide among plates and serve hot.

Enjoy!Nutrition: calories 313, fat 12, fiber 14, carbs 27, protein 44

 Italian Chicken Preparation time: 10 minutes

Cooking time: 16 minutes

Servings: 4Ingredients:

5 chicken thighs

1 tablespoon olive oil

2 garlic cloves, minced

1 tablespoon thyme, chopped

½ cup heavy cream

¾ cup chicken stock

1 teaspoon red pepper flakes, crushed

¼ cup parmesan, grated

½ cup sun dried tomatoes

2 tablespoons basil, chopped

Salt and black pepper to the taste

Directions:

 Season the chicken with salt and hu season, rub with half of the oil and cook in a 350 ° F preheated air fryer for 4 minutes.

 Meanwhile, heat the pot with the remaining oil over medium high heat, add thyme garlic, pepper flakes, sun dried tomatoes, heavy cream, stock, parmesan, salt and pepper, stir, bring to a simmer, take off heat and transfer to a dish that fits your air fryer.

Add chicken thighs on top, introduce in your air fryer and cook at 320 degrees F for 12 minutes.

Divide among plates and serve with basil sprinkled on top.

Enjoy!Nutrition: calories 272, fat 9, fiber 12, carbs 37, protein 23

 Honey Duck BreastPreparation time: 10 minutes

Cooking time: 22 minutes

Servings: 2Ingredients:

1 smoked duck breast, halved

1 teaspoon honey

1 teaspoon tomato paste

1 tablespoon mustard

½ teaspoon apple vinegarDirections:

In a bowl, mix honey with tomato paste, mustard and vinegar, whisk well, add duck breast pieces, toss to coat well, transfer to your air fryer and cook at 370 degrees F for 15 minutes.

Take duck breast out of the fryer, add to honey mix, toss again, return to air fryer and for a duration of 6 minutes boil at 370 degrees.

Divide among plates and serve with a side salad.

Enjoy!Nutrition: calories 274, fat 11, fiber 13, carbs 22, protein 13

 Chinese Duck Legs Preparation time: 10 minutes

Cooking time: 36 minutes

Servings: 2Ingredients:

2 duck legs

2 dried chilies, chopped

1 tablespoon olive oil

2 star anise

1 bunch spring onions, chopped

4 ginger slices

1 tablespoon oyster sauce

1 tablespoon soy sauce

1 teaspoon sesame oil

14 ounces water

1 tablespoon rice wine

Directions:

Over an average heat, add heat to the oven and add chili, star anise, sesame oil, rice wine, ginger, oyster sauce, soy sauce and water, stir and cook for 6 minutes.

Add spring onions and duck legs, toss to coat, transfer to a pan that fits your air fryer, put in your air fryer and cook at 370 degrees F for 30 minutes.

Divide among plates and serve.

Enjoy!Nutrition: calories 300, fat 12, fiber 12, carbs 26, protein 18

 Chinese Stuffed Chicken Preparation time: 10 minutes

Cooking time: 35 minutes

Servings: 8Ingredients:

1 whole chicken

10 wolfberries

2 red chilies, chopped

4 ginger slices

1 yam, cubed

1 teaspoon soy sauce

Salt and white pepper to the taste

3 teaspoons sesame oil

Directions:

Season chicken with salt, pepper, rub with soy sauce and sesame oil and stuff with wolfberries, yam cubes, chilies and ginger.

Place in your air fryer, cook at 400 degrees F for 20 minutes and then at 360 degrees F for 15 minutes.

Carve chicken, divide among plates and serve.

Enjoy!Nutrition: calories 320, fat 12, fiber 17, carbs 22, protein 12

38. Chicken Parmesan Cutlets

Preparation time: 10 minutes
Cooking time: 15 minutes
Servings: 2
Ingredients:
1 cup Panko bread crumbs
2 tablespoons parmesan cheese, grated
¼ teaspoon garlic powder
1 cup white flour
1 egg, whisked
¾ pound skinless, boneless chicken cutlets
Salt and pepper, to taste
½ cup mozzarella, grated
1 cup tomato sauce
1 ½ tablespoons basil, chopped
Directions:
In a bowl, mix garlic powder and parmesan and stir.
Put flour in a second bowl. Put the egg in a third and beat.
Season chicken with salt and pepper.
Dip in flour, then in the egg mix. Finally, coat in panko.
Cook chicken pieces in the air fryer at 360F for 3 minutes on each side.
Transfer chicken to a baking dish.
Add tomato sauce and top with mozzarella.
Cook in the air fryer at 375F for 7 minutes.
Divide among plates, sprinkle basil on top and serve.
Nutrition:
Calories: 304
Fat: 12g
Carb: 22g
Protein: 15g

39. Mexican Chicken Breast

Preparation time: 10 minutes
Cooking time: 20 minutes
Servings: 2
Ingredients:
8 ounces salsa verde
½ tablespoon olive oil
Salt and black pepper, to taste
½ pound boneless, skinless chicken breast
¾ cup Monetary Jack cheese, grated
2 tablespoons cilantro, chopped

½ teaspoon garlic powder
Directions:
Pour salsa verde into a baking dish.
Season chicken with salt, pepper, garlic powder, and brush with olive oil. Place over the salsa verde.
Place baking dish in the air fryer and cook at 380F for 20 minutes.
Sprinkle cheese over the top and cook 2 more minutes.
Serve.
Nutrition:
Calories: 340
Fat: 18g
Carb: 32g
Protein: 18g

40. Turkey and Cream Cheese Breast Pillows

Preparation time: 5 minutes
Cooking time: 10 minutes
Servings: 45
Ingredients:
1 cup of milk with 1 egg inside (put the egg in the cup and then fill with milk)
1/3 cup of water
¼ cup olive oil or oil
1 and ¾ teaspoon of salt
2 tbsp sugar
2 and ½ tbsp dried granular yeast
4 cups of flour
1 egg yolk to brush
2 jars of cream cheese
15 slices of turkey breast cut in 4
Directions:
Mix all the dough ingredients with your hands until it is very smooth. After the ready dough, make small balls and place on a floured surface. Reserve
Open each dough ball with a roller trying to make it square. Cut squares of approximately 10 X 10 cm. Fill with a piece of turkey breast and 1 teaspoon of cream cheese coffee. Close the union of the masses joining the 4 points. Brush with the egg yolk and set aside.
Preheat the air fryer. Set the timer of 5 minutes and the temperature to 200C.
Place 6 units in the basket of the air fryer and bake for 4 or 5 minutes at 180C.
Repeat until all the pillows have finished cooking.
Nutrition:
Calories: 538
Fat: 29.97g
Carbohydrates: 22.69g
Protein: 43.64g
Sugar: 0.56g
Cholesterol: 137mg

41. Chicken Wings

Preparation time: 10 minutes
Cooking time: 25 minutes
Servings: 2
Ingredients:
10 chicken wings (about 700g)
Oil in spay
1 tbsp soy sauce
½ tbsp cornstarch
2 tbsp honey
1 tbsp ground fresh chili paste
1 tbsp minced garlic
½ tsp chopped fresh ginger
1 tbsp lime sumo
½ tbsp salt
2 tbsp chives
Directions:
Dry the chicken with a tea towel. Cover the chicken with the oil spray.
Place the chicken inside the hot air electric fryer, separating the wings towards the edge so that it is not on top of each other. Cook at 200°C until the skin is crispy for about 25 min. Turn them around half the time.
Mix the soy sauce with cornstarch in a small pan. Add honey, chili paste, garlic, ginger, and lime sumo. Simmer until it boils and thickens. Place the chicken in a bowl, add the sauce and cover all the chicken. Sprinkle with chives.
Nutrition:
Calories: 81
Fat: 5.4g
Carbohydrates: 0g
Protein: 7.46g
Sugar: 0g
Cholesterol: 23mg

42. Pickled Poultry

Preparation time: 10 minutes
Cooking time: 25 minutes
Servings: 4
Ingredients:
600g of poultry, without bones or skin
3 white onions, peeled and cut into thin slices
5 garlic cloves, peeled and sliced
3 dl olive oil
1 dl apple cider vinegar
½ l white wine
2 bay leaves
5 g peppercorns
Flour
Pepper
Salt

Directions:

Rub the bird in dice that we will pepper and flour

Put a pan with oil on the fire. When the oil is hot, fry the floured meat dice in it until golden brown. Take them out and reserve, placing them in a clay or oven dish. Strain the oil in which you have fried the meat

Preheat the oven to 170° C

Put the already cast oil in another pan over the fire. Sauté the garlic and onions in it. Add the white wine and let cook about 3 minutes. Remove the pan from the heat, add the vinegar to the oil and wine. Remove, rectify salt, and pour this mixture into the source where you had left the bird dice. Introduce the source in the oven, lower the temperature to 140°C and bake for 1 and ½ hours. Remove the source from the oven and let it stand at room temperature

When the source is cold, put it in the fridge and let it rest a few hours before serving.

Nutrition:

Calories: 232

Fat: 15g

Carbohydrates: 5.89g

Protein: 18.2g

Sugar: 1.72g

Cholesterol: 141mg

43. Cordon Bleu Chicken Breast

Preparation time: 10 minutes

Cooking time: 40 minutes

Servings: 6

Ingredients:

4 flattened chicken breasts

8 slices of ham

16 slices of Swiss cheese

2 tsp fresh thyme

¼ cup flour

1 cup of ground bread

2 tsp melted butter

2 eggs

1 clove garlic finely chopped

pam cooking spray

Directions:

Preheat the air fryer to 350 degrees Fahrenheit (180 °C), set timer to 5 minutes. Then, flatten chicken breasts.

Fill the chicken breasts with two slices of cheese, then 2 slices of ham and finally 2 slices of cheese and roll up. Use a stick if necessary, to save the shape.

Mix the ground bread with the thyme, the garlic finely chopped, with the melted butter and with salt and pepper. Beat the eggs. Season the flour with salt and pepper.

Pass the chicken rolls first through the flour, then through the egg and finally through the breadcrumbs.

Bake until the breasts are cooked, about 20 minutes.

Alternatively, before putting the chicken breasts in the air fryer you can fry them in a little butter and then finish cooking in the air fryer for 13-15 minutes.
Nutrition:
Calories: 387
Fat: 20g
Carbohydrates: 18g
Protein: 33g
Sugar: 0g
Cholesterol: 42mg

44. Fried Chicken

Preparation time: 15 minutes
Cooking time: 25 minutes
Servings: 4
Ingredients:
1kg of chicken chopped into small pieces
Garlic powder
Salt
Ground pepper
1 little grated ginger
1 lemon
Extra virgin olive oil
Directions:
Put the chicken in a large bowl.
Add the lemon juice and pepper.
Add some grated ginger and mix well.
Leave 15 minutes in the refrigerator.
Add now a jet of extra virgin olive oil and mix.
Put the chicken in the air fryer, if it does not fit in a batch, it is put in two.
Select 180 degrees, 25 minutes.
Shake the baskets a few times so that the chicken rotates and is made on all sides.
If you want to pass the chicken for flour, before putting it in the basket and frying, you can do it.
Nutrition:
Calories: 4
Fat: 3.3g
Carbohydrates: 2.3g
Protein: 2.5g
Sugar: 0.1g
Cholesterol: 8.8mg

45. Rolls Stuffed with Broccoli and Carrots with Chicken

Preparation time: 15 minutes
Cooking time: 25 minutes
Servings: 4
Ingredients:
8 sheets of rice pasta

1 chicken breast
1 onion
1 carrot
150g broccolis
1 can of sweet corn
Extra virgin olive oil
Salt
Ground pepper
Soy sauce
1 bag of rice three delicacies
Directions:
Start with the vegetable that you have to cook previously, stop them, peel the carrot.
Cut the carrot and broccoli as small as you can. Add the broccolis and the carrot to a pot with boiling water and let cook a few minutes, they have to be tender, but not too much, that crunch a little.
Drain well and reserve.
Cut the onion into julienne.
Cut the breast into strips.
In the Wok, put some extra virgin olive oil.
Add to the wok when it is hot, the onion and the chicken breast.
Sauté well until the chicken is cooked.
Drain the corn and add to the wok along with the broccolis and the carrot.
Sauté so that the ingredients are mixed.
Add salt, ground pepper and a little soy sauce.
Mix well and let the filling cool.
Hydrate the rice pasta sheets.
Spread on the worktable and distribute the filling between the sheets of rice paste.
Assemble the rolls and paint with a little oil.
Put in the air fryer, those who enter do not pile up.
Select 10 minutes 200 degrees.
When you have all the rolls made, the first ones will have cooled, because to solve it, you now place all the rolls already cooked inside the air fryer, now it does not matter that they are piled up.
Select 180 degrees, 5 minutes.
Make while the rice as indicated by the manufacturer in its bag.
Serve the rice with the rolls.
Nutrition:
Calories: 125
Fat: 4.58g
Carbohydrates: 16.83g
Protein: 4.69g
Sugar: 4.43g
Cholesterol: 0mg

46. Chicken Flutes with Sour Sauce and Guacamole

Preparation time: 15 minutes
Cooking time: 25 minutes
Servings: 4
Ingredients:
8 wheat cakes
1 large roasted breast
Grated cheese
Sour sauce
Guacamole
Extra virgin olive oil
Directions:
Extend the wheat cakes.
Stuffed with grated cheese and well-roasted chicken breast.
Form the flues and paint with extra virgin olive oil.
Place in batches in the air fryer and select 180 degrees, 5 minutes on each side or until you see the flutes golden.
Serve with sour sauce and guacamole.
Nutrition:
Calories: 325
Fat: 7g
Carbohydrates: 45g
Protein: 13g
Sugar: 7g
Cholesterol: 0mg

47. Spicy Chicken Strips

Preparation time: 5 minutes
Cooking time: 12 minutes
Servings: 5
Ingredients:
1 cup buttermilk
1½ tbsp hot pepper sauce
1 tsp salt
½ tsp black pepper, divided
1 pound boneless and skinless chicken breasts, cut into ¾ inch strips
¾ cup panko breadcrumbs
½ tsp salt
¼ tsp hot pepper, or to taste
1 tbsp olive oil
Directions:
Put the buttermilk, hot sauce, salt and ¼ teaspoon of black pepper in shallow bowl. Add chicken strips and refrigerate for at least two hours. Put breadcrumbs, salt, and the remaining black pepper and hot pepper in another bowl; Add and stir the oil.
Remove the chicken strips from the marinade and discard the marinade. Put the strips, few at the same time, to the crumb mixture. Press the crumbs to the strips to achieve a uniform and firm cover.

Put half of the strips in single layer inside the basket. Cook at a temperature of 350°F for 12 minutes. Cook the rest when the first batch is cooked.
Nutrition:
Calories: 207
Fat: 9g
Carbohydrates: 5g
Protein: 25g
Sugar: 0g
Cholesterol: 0mg

48. Spinach Stuffed Chicken Breasts

Servings: 2
Preparation Time: 15 minutes
Cooking Time: 30 minutes
Ingredients
1 tablespoon olive oil
1¾ ounces fresh spinach
¼ cup ricotta cheese, shredded
2, 4-ouncesskinless, boneless chicken breasts
Salt and ground black pepper, as required
2 tablespoons cheddar cheese, grated
¼ teaspoon paprika
Instructions
In a medium skillet, add the oil over medium heat and cook until heated.
Add the spinach and cook for about 3-4 minutes.
Stir in the ricotta and cook for about 40-60 seconds.
Remove the skillet from heat and set aside to cool.
Cut slits into the chicken breasts about ¼-inch apart but not all the way through.
Stuff each chicken breast with the spinach mixture.
Sprinkle each chicken breast evenly with salt and black pepper and then with cheddar cheese and paprika.
Set the temperature of Air Fryer to 390 degrees F. Grease an Air Fryer basket.
Arrange chicken breasts into the prepared basket in a single layer.
Air Fry for about 20-25 minutes.
Remove from Air Fryer and transfer the chicken breasts onto a serving platter.
Serve hot.
Nutrition:
Calories: 279
Carbohydrate: 2.7g
Protein: 31.4g
Fat: 16g
Sugar: 0.3g
Sodium: 220mg

49. Cheese Stuffed Chicken Breasts

Servings: 4
Preparation Time: 15 minutes
Cooking Time: 15 minutes
Ingredients
2, 8-ouncesskinless, boneless chicken breast fillets
Salt and ground black pepper, as required
4 Brie cheese slices
1 tablespoon fresh chive, minced
4 cured ham slices
Instructions
Cut each chicken fillet in 2 equal-sized pieces.
Carefully, make a slit in each chicken piece horizontally about ¼-inch from the edge.
Open each chicken piece and season with the salt and black pepper.
Place 1 cheese slice in the open area of each chicken piece and sprinkle with chives.
Close the chicken pieces and wrap each one with a ham slice.
Set the temperature of Air Fryer to 355 degrees F. Grease an Air Fryer basket.
Arrange the wrapped chicken pieces into the prepared Air Fryer basket.
Air Fry for about 15 minutes.
Remove from Air Fryer and transfer the chicken fillets onto a serving platter.
Serve hot.
Nutrition:
Calories: 376
Carbohydrate: 1.5g
Protein: 44.5g
Fat: 20.2g
Sugar: 0g
Sodium: 639mg

50. Bacon Wrapped Chicken Breasts

Servings: 4
Preparation Time: 20 minutes
Cooking Time: 23 minutes
Ingredients
1 tablespoon palm sugar
6-7 Fresh basil leaves
2 tablespoons fish sauce
2 tablespoons water
2, 8-ounceschicken breasts, cut each breast in half horizontally
Salt and ground black pepper, as required
12 bacon strips
1½ teaspoon honey
Instructions

In a small heavy-bottomed pan, add palm sugar over medium-low heat and cook for about 2-3 minutes or until caramelized, stirring continuously.

Add the basil, fish sauce and water and stir to combine.

Remove from heat and transfer the sugar mixture into a large bowl.

Sprinkle each chicken breast with salt and black pepper.

Add the chicken pieces in sugar mixture and coat generously.

Refrigerate to marinate for about 4-6 hours.

Set the temperature of Air Fryer to 365 degrees F. Grease an Air Fryer basket.

Wrap each chicken piece with 3 bacon strips.

Coat each piece slightly with honey.

Arrange chicken pieces into the prepared Air Fryer basket.

Air Fry for about 20 minutes, flipping once halfway through.

Remove from Air Fryer and transfer the chicken pieces onto a serving platter.

Serve hot.

Nutrition:

Calories: 365

Carbohydrate: 2.7g

Protein: 30.2g

Fat: 24.8g

Sugar: 2.1g

Sodium: 1300mg

51. Buffalo Chicken Tenders

Servings: 3

Preparation Time: 20 minutes

Cooking Time: 12 minutes

Ingredients

1 tablespoon water

1 large egg

16 ounces boneless, skinless chicken breasts, sliced into tenders

½ cup pork rinds, crushed

½ cup unflavored whey protein powder

½ teaspoon garlic powder

Salt and ground black pepper, as required

2 tablespoons butter, melted

¼ cup buffalo wing sauce

Instructions

In a large bowl, add the water, and egg. Beat until well combined.

Add the chicken and generously coat with egg mixture.

Place the chicken in a colander to drain completely.

In a shallow bowl, mix together the pork rinds, protein powder, garlic powder, salt, and black pepper.

Coat chicken tenders with the pork rinds mixture.

Set the temperature of Air Fryer to 400 degrees F. Grease an Air Fryer basket.

Arrange chicken tenders into the prepared Air Fryer basket and drizzle with the melted butter.

Air Fry for about 10-12 minutes.
Remove from Air Fryer and transfer the chicken tenders into a bowl.
Place with the buffalo sauce and toss to coat well.
Serve immediately.
Nutrition:
Calories: 292
Carbohydrate: 0.9g
Protein: 43.6g
Fat: 12.9g
Sugar: 0.2g
Sodium: 261mg

52. Crispy Chicken Tenders

Servings: 3
Preparation Time: 20 minutes
Cooking Time: 30 minutes
Ingredients
2, 6-ouncesboneless, skinless chicken breasts, pounded into ½-inch thickness and cut into tenders
¾ cup buttermilk
1½ teaspoons Worcestershire sauce, divided
½ teaspoon smoked paprika, divided
Salt and ground black pepper, as required
½ cup all-purpose flour
1½ cups panko breadcrumbs
¼ cup Parmesan cheese, finely grated
2 tablespoons butter, melted
2 large eggs
 Instructions
In a large bowl, mix together buttermilk, ¾ teaspoon of Worcestershire sauce, ¼ teaspoon of paprika, salt, and black pepper.
Add in the chicken tenders and refrigerate overnight.
In another bowl, mix together the flour, remaining paprika, salt, and black pepper.
Place the remaining Worcestershire sauce and eggs in a third bowl and beat until well combined.
Mix well the panko, Parmesan, and butter in a fourth bowl.
Remove the chicken tenders from bowl and discard the buttermilk.
Coat the chicken tenders with flour mixture, then dip into egg mixture and finally coat with the panko mixture.
Set the temperature of air fryer to 400 degrees F. Grease an air fryer basket.
Arrange chicken tenders into the prepared air fryer basket in 2 batches in a single layer.
Air fry for about 13-15 minutes, flipping once halfway through.
Remove from air fryer and transfer the chicken tenders onto a serving platter.
Serve hot.

Nutrition
Calories: 654
Carbohydrate: 28g
Protein: 454g
Fat: 25.5g
Sugar: 3.9g
Sodium: 399mg

53. Simple Chicken Wings

Servings: 2
Preparation Time: 10 minutes
Cooking Time: 25 minutes
Ingredients
1 pound chicken wings
Salt and ground black pepper, as required
Instructions
Set the temperature of Air Fryer to 380 degrees F. Generously, grease an Air Fryer basket.
Sprinkle the chicken wings evenly with salt and black pepper.
Arrange chicken wings into the prepared Air Fryer basket in a single layer.
Air Fry for about 25 minutes, flip the wings once halfway through.
Remove from Air Fryer and transfer the chicken wings onto a serving platter. Serve hot.
Nutrition
Calories: 431
Carbohydrate: 0g
Protein: 65.6g
Fat: 16.8g
Sugar: 0g
Sodium: 273mg

54. Crispy Chicken Wings

Servings: 2
Preparation Time: 20 minutes
Cooking Time: 25 minutes
Ingredients
2 lemongrass stalk, white portion, minced
1 onion, finely chopped
1 tablespoon soy sauce
1½ tablespoons honey
Salt and ground white pepper, as required
1 pound chicken wings, rinsed and trimmed
½ cup cornstarch
Instructions

In a bowl, mix together the lemongrass, onion, soy sauce, honey, salt, and white pepper.

Add the wings and generously coat with marinade.

Cover and refrigerate to marinate overnight.

Set the temperature of Air Fryer to 355 degrees F. Grease an Air Fryer basket.

Remove the chicken wings from marinade and coat with the cornstarch.

Arrange chicken wings into the prepared Air Fryer basket in a single layer.

Air Fry for about 25 minutes, flipping once halfway through.

Remove from Air Fryer and transfer the chicken wings onto a serving platter.

Serve hot.

Nutrition:

Calories: 724

Carbohydrate: 56.9g

Protein: 43.5g

Fat: 36.2g

Sugar: 15.4g

Sodium: 702mg

55. BBQ Chicken Wings

Servings: 4

Preparation Time: 10 minutes

Cooking Time: 30 minutes

Ingredients

2 pounds chicken wings, cut into drumettes and flats

½ cup BBQ sauce

Instructions

Set the temperature of Air Fryer to 380 degrees F. Grease an Air Fryer basket.

Arrange chicken wings into the prepared Air Fryer basket in a single layer.

Air Fry for about 24 minutes, flipping once halfway through.

Now, set the temperature of Air Fryer to 400 degrees F.

Air Fry for about 6 minutes.

Remove from Air Fryer and transfer the chicken wings into a bowl.

Drizzle with the BBQ sauce and toss to coat well.

Serve immediately.

Nutrition

Calories: 478

Carbohydrate: 11.3g

Protein: 65.6g

Fat: 16.9g

Sugar: 8.1g

Sodium: 545mg

56. Buffalo Chicken Wings

Servings: 6
Preparation Time: 20 minutes
Cooking Time: 22 minutes
Ingredients
2 pounds chicken wings, cut into drumettes and flats
1 teaspoon chicken seasoning
1 teaspoon garlic powder
Ground black pepper, to taste
1 tablespoon olive oil
¼ cup red hot sauce
2 tablespoons low-sodium soy sauce
Instructions
Set the temperature of Air Fryer to 400 degrees F. Grease an Air Fryer basket.
Sprinkle each chicken wing evenly with chicken seasoning, garlic powder, and
black pepper.
Arrange chicken wings into the prepared Air Fryer basket in a single layer and
drizzle with oil.
Air Fry for about 10 minutes, shaking the basket once halfway through.
Remove from Air Fryer and transfer the chicken wings into a bowl.
Drizzle with the red hot sauce, oil, and soy sauce. Toss to coat well.
Place chicken wings for the second time into the Air Fryer basket in a single layer.
Air Fry for about 7-12 minutes at the same temperature.
Remove from Air Fryer and transfer the chicken wings onto a serving platter.
Serve hot.
Nutrition:
Calories: 311
Carbohydrate: 0.6g
Protein: 44g
Fat: 13.6g
Sugar: 0.3g
Sodium: 491mg
>-Note: Buffalo Chicken Wings – When red hot sauce is used with chicken
wings, it's called Buffalo Chicken Wings.

57. Sweet Chicken Kabobs

Servings: 3
Preparation Time: 20 minutes
Cooking Time: 14 minutes
Ingredients
4 scallions, chopped
1 tablespoon fresh ginger, finely grated
4 garlic cloves, minced
½ cup pineapple juice
½ cup soy sauce
¼ cup sesame oil

2 teaspoons sesame seeds, toasted
A pinch of black pepper
1 pound chicken tenders
Instructions
In a large baking dish, mix together the scallion, ginger, garlic, pineapple juice, soy sauce, oil, sesame seeds, and black pepper.
Thread chicken tenders onto the pre-soaked wooden skewers.
Add the skewers into the baking dish and evenly coat with marinade.
Cover and refrigerate for about 2 hours or overnight.
Set the temperature of Air Fryer to 390 degrees F. Grease an Air Fryer basket.
Place chicken skewers into the prepared Air Fryer basket in 2 batches.
Air Fry for about 5-7 minutes.
Remove from Air Fryer and transfer the chicken skewers onto a serving platter.
Serve hot.
Nutrition:
Calories: 392
Carbohydrate: 9.9g
Protein: 35.8g
Fat: 23g
Sugar: 4.1g
Sodium: 1800mg

58. Chicken & Scallion Kabobs

Servings: 4
Preparation Time: 20 minutes
Cooking Time: 24 minutes
Ingredients
¼ cup light soy sauce
1 tablespoon mirin
1 teaspoon garlic salt
1 teaspoon sugar
4, 4-ouncesskinless, boneless chicken thighs, cubed into 1-inch size
5 scallions, cut into 1-inch pieces lengthwise
Instructions
In a baking dish, mix together the soy sauce, mirin, garlic salt, and sugar.
Thread chicken and scallions onto pre-soaked wooden skewers.
Place skewers into the baking dish and generously coat with marinade.
Cover and refrigerate for about 3 hours.
Set the temperature of Air Fryer to 355 degrees F. Grease an Air Fryer basket.
Arrange skewers into the prepared Air Fryer basket in 2 batches in a single layer.
Air Fry for about 10-12 minutes.
Once done, remove from Air Fryer and transfer the chicken skewers onto a serving platter.
Serve hot.
Nutrition
Calories: 161

Carbohydrate: 6.9g
Protein: 26.2g
Fat: 4.1g
Sugar: 4g
Sodium: 781mg

59. Chicken & Veggie Kabobs

Servings: 3
Preparation Time: 20 minutes
Cooking Time: 30 minutes
Ingredients
1 lb. skinless, boneless chicken thighs, cut into cubes
½ cup plain Greek yogurt
1 tablespoon olive oil
2 teaspoons curry powder
½ teaspoon smoked paprika
¼ teaspoon cayenne pepper
Salt, to taste
2 small bell peppers, seeded and cut into large chunks
1 large red onion, cut into large chunks
Instructions
In a bowl, add the chicken, oil, yogurt, and spices and mix until well combined
Refrigerate to marinate for about 2 hours.
Thread the chicken cubes, bell pepper and onion onto pre-soaked wooden skewers.
Set the temperature of Air Fryer to 360 degrees F. Grease an Air Fryer basket.
Arrange chicken skewers into the prepared Air Fryer basket in 2 batches.
Air Fry for about 15 minutes.
Remove from Air Fryer and transfer the chicken skewers onto a serving platter.
Serve hot.
Nutrition
Calories: 222
Carbohydrate: 8.7g
Protein: 27.9g
Fat: 8.2g
Sugar: 5.3g
Sodium: 104mg

60. Jerk Chicken, Pineapple & Veggie Kabobs

Servings: 8
Preparation Time: 20 minutes
Cooking Time: 18 minutes
Ingredients
8, 4-ouncesboneless, skinless chicken thigh fillets, trimmed and cut into cubes
1 tablespoon jerk seasoning

2 large zucchini, sliced
8 ounces white mushrooms, stems removed
Salt and ground black pepper, as required
1, 20-ouncescan pineapple chunks, drained
1 tablespoon jerk sauce
Instructions
In a bowl, mix together the chicken cubes and jerk seasoning.
Cover the bowl and refrigerate overnight.
Sprinkle the zucchini slices, and mushrooms evenly with salt and black pepper.
Thread the chicken, vegetables and pineapple onto greased metal skewers.
Set the temperature of Air Fryer to 370 degrees F. Grease an Air Fryer basket.
Arrange skewers into the prepared Air Fryer basket in 2 batches.
Air Fry for about 8-9 minutes, flipping and coating with jerk sauce once halfway through.
Remove from Air Fryer and transfer the chicken skewers onto a serving platter.
Serve hot.
Nutrition
Calories: 274
Carbohydrate: 14.1g
Protein: 35.1g
Fat: 8.7g
Sugar: 9.9g
Sodium: 150mg

61. Curried Chicken

Servings: 3
Preparation Time: 15 minutes
Cooking Time: 18 minutes
Ingredients
1-pound boneless chicken, cubed
1 tablespoon light soy sauce
½ tablespoon cornstarch
1 egg
2 tablespoons olive oil
1 medium yellow onion, thinly sliced
1 green chili, chopped
3 teaspoons garlic, minced
1 teaspoon fresh ginger, grated
5 curry leaves
1 teaspoon curry powder
1 tablespoon chili sauce
1 teaspoon sugar
Salt and ground black pepper, as required
½ cup evaporated milk
Instructions

In a bowl, add the chicken cubes, soy sauce, cornstarch, and egg and mix until well combined.

Cover the bowl and place at room temperature for about 1 hour.

Remove chicken cubes from the bowl and with paper towels, pat them dry.

Set the temperature of Air Fryer to 390 degrees F. Grease an Air Fryer basket.

Arrange chicken cubes into the prepared Air Fryer basket.

Air Fry for about 10 minutes.

Remove chicken cubes from the Air fryer and set aside.

In a medium skillet, add the oil over medium heat and cook until heated.

Add the onion, green chili, garlic, ginger, and curry leaves. Sauté for about 3-4 minutes.

Add the chicken cubes, curry powder, chili sauce, sugar, salt, and black pepper and mix until well combined.

Stir in the evaporated milk and cook for about 3-4 minutes.

Remove from heat and transfer the chicken mixture into a serving bowl.

Serve hot.

Nutrition:

Calories: 363

Carbohydrate: 10g

Protein: 37.1g

Fat: 19g

Sugar: 0.8g

Sodium: 789mg

62. Chicken with Apple

Servings: 2

Preparation Time: 20 minutes

Cooking Time: 20 minutes

Ingredients

1 shallot, thinly sliced

1 tablespoon fresh ginger, finely grated

1 teaspoon fresh thyme, minced

½ cup apple cider

2 tablespoons maple syrup

Salt and ground black pepper, as required

2, 4-ouncesboneless, skinless chicken thighs, sliced into chunks

1 large apple, cored and cubed

Instructions

In a bowl, mix together the shallot, ginger, thyme, apple cider, maple syrup, salt, and black pepper.

Add the chicken pieces and generously mix with the marinade.

Refrigerate to marinate for about 6-8 hours.

Set the temperature of Air Fryer to 390 degrees F. Grease an Air Fryer basket.

Place the chicken pieces and cubed apple into the prepared Air Fryer basket.

Air Fry for about 20 minutes, flipping once halfway.

Remove from Air Fryer and transfer the chicken mixture onto a serving platter.

Serve hot.
Nutrition:
Calories: 299
Carbohydrate: 39.9g
Protein: 26.2g
Fat: 4.6g
Sugar: 30.4g
Sodium: 125mg

63. Chicken with Carrots

Servings: 2
Preparation Time: 15 minutes
Cooking Time: 25 minutes
Ingredients
1 carrot, peeled and thinly sliced
Salt and ground black pepper, as required
2 tablespoons butter
2, 4-ounceschicken breast halves
1 tablespoon fresh rosemary, chopped
2 tablespoons fresh lemon juice
Instructions
Arrange 2 square-shaped parchment papers onto a smooth surface.
Place carrot slices evenly in the center of each parchment paper.
Place ½ tablespoon of butter over carrot slices and sprinkle with salt and black pepper.
Arrange 1 chicken breast over carrot slices in each parcel.
Top each chicken breast evenly with rosemary and drizzle with lemon juice.
Top with the remaining butter.
Seal each parchment paper by folding all four corners.
Set the temperature of Air Fryer to 375 degrees F.
Arrange the chicken parcels into an Air Fryer basket.
Air Fry for about 20-25 minutes.
Remove from Air Fryer and transfer the chicken mixture onto a serving platter.
Serve hot.
Nutrition:
Calories: 339
Carbohydrate: 4.4g
Protein: 33.4g
Fat: 20.3g
Sugar: 18g
Sodium: 282mg

64. Chicken with Veggies

Servings: 2
Preparation Time: 20 minutes
Cooking Time: 45 minutes
Ingredients
2 garlic cloves, minced
2 tablespoons chicken broth
2 tablespoons red wine vinegar
2 tablespoons olive oil
1 tablespoon Dijon mustard
1/8 teaspoon dried thyme
1/8 teaspoon dried basil
4 small artichoke hearts, quartered
4 fresh large button mushrooms, quartered
½ small onion, cut in large chunks
Salt and ground black pepper, as required
2 skinless, boneless chicken breasts
2 tablespoons fresh parsley, chopped
Instructions
Grease a small baking dish that will fit in the cooking basket of Air Fryer.
In a small bowl, mix together the garlic, broth, vinegar, olive oil, mustard, thyme, and basil.
In the prepared baking dish, add the artichokes, mushrooms, onions, salt, and black pepper and mix well
Now, place the chicken breasts on top of veggie mixture in a single layer.
Spread half of the mustard mixture evenly over chicken breasts.
Set the temperature of Air Fryer to 350 degrees F.
Arrange the baking dish into an Air Fryer cooking basket.
Air Fry for about 23 minutes.
Coat the chicken breasts with the remaining mustard mixture and flip the side.
Air Fry for about 22 minutes.
Remove from Air Fryer and transfer the chicken mixture onto a serving platter.
Garnish with parsley and serve hot.
Nutrition:
Calories: 448
Carbohydrate: 39.1g
Protein: 38.5g
Fat: 19.1g
Sugar: 5g
Sodium: 566mg
>-Note: If you want your chicken to be crispy, then set the temperature of air fryer to 375 degrees F.

65. Chicken Chilaquiles

Servings: 3
Preparation Time: 20 minutes
Cooking Time: 50 minutes
Ingredients
1, 8-ouncesskinless, boneless chicken breast
2 bay leaves
1 small yellow onion, chopped
3 garlic cloves, chopped
½ of poblano pepper
1, 14½-ouncecan diced tomatoes
1, 10-ouncescan Rotel tomatoes
Salt, to taste
10 corn tortillas, cut into diamond slices
1 tablespoon olive oil
4 tablespoons feta cheese, crumbled
¼ cup sour cream
2 red onions, sliced
Instructions
In a pan of water, add the chicken, and bay leaves and cook for about 20 minutes.
With a slotted spoon, transfer chicken breasts into a bowl and set aside to cool.
Shred the chicken using 2 forks.
In a food processor, add the onion, garlic, poblano pepper, and both cans of tomatoes and pulse until smooth.
Transfer the sauce into a skillet over medium-high heat and bring to a boil.
Reduce the heat to medium-low and cook for about 10 minutes.
Season with salt and remove from the heat.
Set the temperature of Air Fryer to 400 degrees F. Grease an Air Fryer basket.
In a bowl, add the tortilla slices, oil and salt and toss to coat well.
Arrange tortilla slices into the prepared Air Fryer basket in 2 batches in a single layer.
Air Fry for about 10 minutes.
Transfer the tortilla slices into the serving bowl.
Add the sauce, cheese, and sour cream and mix well.
Top with the chicken, and red onions and serve.
Nutrition
Calories: 375
Carbohydrate: 42.8g
Protein: 25.9g
Fat: 12.7g
Sugar: 7g
Sodium: 536mg

66. Chicken with Broccoli & Rice

Servings: 6
Preparation Time: 20 minutes
Cooking Time: 15 minutes
Ingredients
3 tablespoons dried parsley, crushed
1 tablespoon onion powder
1 tablespoon garlic powder
½ teaspoon red chili powder
½ teaspoon paprika
2 pounds boneless, skinless chicken breasts, sliced
3 cups instant white rice
¾ cup cream soup
3 cups small broccoli florets
1/3 cup butter
3 cups water
Instructions
Mix together the parsley and spices in a large bowl.
Add the chicken slices and generously coat with spice mixture.
Arrange 6 large pieces of foil onto a smooth surface.
Place ½ cup of rice over each foil piece, followed by 1/6 of chicken, 2 tablespoons of cream soup, ½ cup of broccoli, 1 tablespoon of butter, and ½ cup of water.
Fold the foil tightly to seal the rice mixture.
Set the temperature of Air Fryer to 390 degrees F.
Arrange the foil packets into an Air Fryer basket.
Air Fry for about 15 minutes.
Remove from Air Fryer and carefully, transfer the rice mixture onto serving plates.
Serve hot.
Nutrition
Calories: 583
Carbohydrate: 65.6g
Protein: 42.7g
Fat: 23.1g
Sugar: 1.6g
Sodium: 374mg

67. Chicken with Veggies & Rice

Servings: 3
Preparation Time: 15 minutes
Cooking Time: 20 minutes
Ingredients
3 cups cold boiled white rice
6 tablespoons soy sauce
1 tablespoon vegetable oil

1 cup cooked chicken, diced
½ cup frozen carrots
½ cup frozen peas
½ cup onion, chopped
Instructions
In a large bowl, add the rice, soy sauce, and oil and mix thoroughly.
Add the remaining ingredients and mix until well combined.
Transfer the rice mixture into a 7" nonstick pan.
Arrange the pan into an Air Fryer basket.
Set the temperature of Air Fryer to 360 degrees F.
Air Fry for about 20 minutes.
Remove the pan from Air Fryer and transfer the rice mixture onto serving plates.
Serve immediately.
Nutrition:
Calories: 405
Carbohydrate: 63g
Protein: 21.7g
Fat: 6.4g
Sugar: 3.5g
Sodium: 1500mg

Fish and Seafood Recipes
68.   Cajun Style Shrimp

Preparation time: 3 minutes
Cooking time: 10 minutes
Servings: 2
Ingredients:
6g of salt
2g smoked paprika
2g garlic powder
2g Italian seasoning
2g chili powder
1g onion powder
1g cayenne pepper
1g black pepper
1g dried thyme
454g large shrimp, peeled and unveiled
30 ml of olive oil
Lime wedges, to serve
Directions:
Select Preheat, in the air fryer, set the temperature to 190°C and press Start/Pause.
Combine all seasonings in a large bowl. Set aside
Mix the shrimp with olive oil until they are evenly coated.
Sprinkle the dressing mixture over the shrimp and stir until well coated.
Place the shrimp in the preheated air fryer.
Select Shrimp set the time to 5 minutes and press Start/Pause.
Shake the baskets in the middle of cooking.
Serve with pieces of lime.
Nutrition:
Calories: 126
Fat: 6g
Carbohydrates: 2g
Proteins: 33g
Cholesterol: 199mg
Sodium: 231mg

69. Crab Cakes

Preparation time: 10 minutes
Cooking time: 40 minutes
Servings: 2
Ingredients:
For crab cakes:
1 large egg, beaten
17g of mayonnaise
11g Dijon mustard
5 ml Worcestershire sauce
2g Old Bay seasoning

2g of salt
A pinch of white pepper
A pinch of cayenne
26g celery, finely diced
45g red pepper, finely diced
8g fresh parsley, finely chopped
227g of crab meat
28g breadcrumbs
Nonstick Spray Oil
Remodeled:
55g of mayonnaise
15g capers, washed and drained
5g sweet pickles, chopped
5g red onion, finely chopped
8 ml of lemon juice
8g Dijon mustard
Salt and pepper to taste
Directions:
Mix the ingredients of remodeled until everything is well incorporated. Set aside
Beat the egg, mayonnaise, mustard, Worcestershire sauce, Old Bay seasoning, salt, white pepper, cayenne pepper, celery, pepper, and parsley.
Gently stir the crab meat in the egg mixture and stir it until well mixed.
Sprinkle the breadcrumbs over the crab mixture and fold them gently until the breadcrumbs cover every corner.
Shape the crab mixture into 4 cakes and chill in the fridge for 30 minutes.
Select Preheat in the air fryer and press Start/Pause.
Place a sheet of baking paper in the basket of the preheated air fryer. Sprinkle the crab cakes with cooking spray and place them gently on the paper.
Cook the crab cakes at 205°C for 8 minutes until golden brown.
Flip crab cakes during cooking.
Serve with remodeled.
Nutrition:
Calories: 110
Fat: 6.5g
Carbohydrates: 5.5g
Protein: 7g
Sugar: 2g

70. Tuna Pie

Preparation time: 10 minutes
Cooking time: 30 minutes
Servings: 4
Ingredients:
2 hard-boiled eggs
2 tuna cans
200 ml fried tomato
1 sheet of broken dough.
Directions:

Cut the eggs into small pieces and mix with the tuna and tomato.
Spread the sheet of broken dough and cut into two equal squares.
Put the mixture of tuna, eggs, and tomato on one of the squares.
Cover with the other, join at the ends and decorate with leftover little pieces.
Preheat the air fryer a few minutes at 1800C.
Enter in the air fryer basket and set the timer for 15 minutes at 1800C.
Nutrition:
Calories: 244
Fat: 13.67g
Carbohydrates: 21.06g
Protein: 8.72g
Sugar: 0.22g
Cholesterol: 59mg

71. Tuna Puff Pastry

Preparation time: 5 minutes
Cooking time: 15 minutes
Servings: 2
Ingredients:
2 square puff pastry dough, bought ready
1 egg (white and yolk separated)
½ cup tuna tea
½ cup chopped parsley tea
½ cup chopped tea olives
Salt and pepper to taste
Directions:
Preheat the air fryer. Set the timer of 5 minutes and the temperature to 200C.
Mix the tuna with olives and parsley. Season to taste and set aside. Place half of
the filling in each dough and fold in half. Brush with egg white and close gently.
After closing, make two small cuts at the top of the air outlet. Brush with the egg
yolk.
Place in the basket of the air fryer. Set the time to 10 minutes and press the
power button.
Nutrition:
Calories: 291
Fat: 16g
Carbohydrates: 26g
Protein: 8g
Sugar: 0g
Cholesterol: 0

72. Cajun Style Catfish

Preparation time: 3 minutes
Cooking time: 7 minutes
Servings: 2
Ingredients:
5g of paprika
3g garlic powder
2g onion powder

2g ground dried thyme

1g ground black pepper

1g cayenne pepper

1g dried basil

1g dried oregano

2 catfish fillets (6 oz)

Nonstick Spray Oil

Direction:

Preheat the air fryer for a few minutes. Set the temperature to 175°C.

Mix all seasonings in a bowl.

Cover the fish generously on each side with the dressing mixture.

Spray each side of the fish with oil spray and place it in the preheated air fryer.

Select Marine Food and press Start /Pause.

Remove carefully when you finish cooking and serve on semolina.

Nutrition:

Calories: 228

Fat; 13g

Carbohydrates: 0g

Protein: 20g

Sugar: 0g

Cholesterol: 71mg

73. Tuna Chipotle

Preparation time: 5 minutes

Cooking time: 8 minutes

Servings: 2

Ingredients:

142g tuna

45g chipotle sauce

4 slices of white bread

2 slices of pepper jack cheese

Directions:

Preheat the air fryer set the temperature to 160°C.

Mix the tuna and chipotle until combined.

Spread half of the chipotle tuna mixture on each of the 2 slices of bread.

Add a slice of pepper jack cheese on each and close with the remaining 2 slices of bread, making 2 sandwiches.

Place the sandwiches in the preheated air fryer. Set the timer to 8 minutes.

Cut diagonally and serve.

Nutrition:

. Calories: 121

Fat: 4g

Carbohydrates: 2g

Protein: 16g

Sugar: 0g

Cholesterol: 36mg

74. Fish Tacos

Preparation time: 10 minutes

Cooking time: 7 minutes
Servings: 4-5
Ingredients:
454g of tilapia, cut into strips of
38 mm thick
52g yellow cornmeal
1g ground cumin
1g chili powder
2g garlic powder
1g onion powder
3g of salt
1g black pepper
Nonstick Spray Oil
Corn tortillas, to serve
Tartar sauce, to serve
Lime wedges, to serve
Directions:
Cut the tilapia into strips 38 mm thick.
Mix cornmeal and seasonings in a shallow dish.
Cover the fish strips with seasoned cornmeal. Set aside in the fridge.
Preheat the air fryer for 5 minutes. Set the temperature to 170°C.
Sprinkle the fish coated with oil spray and place it in the preheated air fryer.
Put the fish in the air fryer, set the timer to 7 minutes.
Turn the fish halfway through cooking.
Serve the fish in corn tortillas with tartar sauce and a splash of lemon.
Nutrition:
Calories: 108
Fat: 26g
Carbohydrates: 11g
Protein: 9g
Sugar: 0g
Cholesterol: 56mg

75. Delicious Prawns and Sweet Potatoes

Preparation time: 20 minutes
Cooking time: 20 minutes
Servings: 4
Ingredients:
1 shallot, chopped
1 red chili pepper, seeded and chopped finely
12 king prawns, peeled and deveined
5 large sweet potatoes, peeled and cut into slices
4 lemongrass stalks
2 tablespoons dried rosemary
1/3 cup olive oil, divided
4 garlic cloves, minced
Smoked paprika, to taste
1 tablespoon honey

Directions:

Preheat the Air fryer to 355 o F and grease an Air fryer basket.

Mix ¼ cup of the olive oil, shallot, red chili pepper, garlic and paprika in a bowl. Add prawns and coat evenly with the mixture.

Thread the prawns onto lemongrass stalks and refrigerate to marinate for about 3 hours.

Mix sweet potatoes, honey and rosemary in a bowl and toss to coat well.

Arrange the potatoes in the Air fryer basket and cook for about 15 minutes.

Remove the sweet potatoes from the Air fryer and set the Air fryer to 390 degrees F.

Place the prawns in the Air fryer basket and cook for about 5 minutes.

Dish out in a bowl and serve with sweet potatoes.

Nutrition:

Calories: 285, Fats: 3.8g, Carbohydrates: 51.6g, Sugar: 5.8g, Proteins: 10.5g, Sodium: 235mg

76. Nutritious Salmon and Veggie Patties

Preparation time: 15 minutes

Cooking time: 7 minutes

Servings: 6

Ingredients:

3 large russet potatoes, boiled and mashed

1 (6-ounce) salmon fillet

1 egg

¾ cup frozen vegetables, parboiled and drained

1 cup breadcrumbs

2 tablespoons dried parsley, chopped

1 teaspoon dried dill, chopped

Salt and freshly ground pepper, to taste

¼ cup olive oil

Directions:

Preheat the Air fryer to 355 o F and line a pan with foil paper.

Place salmon in the Air fryer basket and cook for about 5 minutes.

Dish out the salmon in a large bowl and flake with a fork.

Mix potatoes, egg, parboiled vegetables, parsley, dill, salt and black pepper until well combined.

Make 6 equal sized patties from the mixture and coat the patties evenly with breadcrumbs.

Drizzle with the olive oil and arrange the patties in the pan.

Transfer into the Air fryer basket and cook for about 12 minutes, flipping once in between.

Nutrition:

Calories: 334, Fat: 12.1g, Carbohydrates: 45.1g, Sugar: 4g, Protein: 12.6g, Sodium: 175mg

77. Cod Cakes

Preparation time: 15 minutes

Cooking time: 14 minutes

Servings 4

Ingredients:

1 pound cod fillets

1 egg

1/3 cup coconut, grated and divided

1 scallion, chopped finely

2 tablespoons fresh parsley, chopped

1 teaspoon fresh lime zest, grated finely

1 teaspoon red chili paste

Salt, to taste

1 tablespoon fresh lime juice

Directions:

Preheat the Air fryer to 375 o F and grease an Air fryer basket.

Put cod filets, lime zest, egg, chili paste, salt and lime juice in a food processor and pulse until smooth.

Transfer the cod mixture to a bowl and add 2 tablespoons coconut, scallion and parsley.

Make 12 equal sized round cakes from the mixture.

Put the remaining coconut in a shallow dish and coat the cod cakes in it.

Arrange 6 cakes in the Air fryer basket and cook for about 7 minutes.

Repeat with the remaining cod cakes and serve warm.

Nutrition:

Calories: 171, Fat: 3.3g, Carbohydrates: 16.1g, Sugar: 13.2g, Protein: 19g, Sodium: 115mg

78. Ham-Wrapped Prawns with Roasted Pepper Chutney

Preparation time: 15 minutes

Cooking time: 13 minutes

Servings: 4

Ingredients:

1 large red bell pepper

8 king prawns, peeled and deveined

4 ham slices, halved

1 garlic clove, minced

1 tablespoon olive oil

½ tablespoon paprika

Salt and freshly ground black pepper, to taste

Directions:

Preheat the Air fryer to 375 o F and grease an Air fryer basket.

Place the bell pepper in the Air fryer basket and cook for about 10 minutes.

Dish out the bell pepper into a bowl and keep aside, covered for about 15 minutes.

Now, peel the bell pepper and remove the stems and seeds and chop it.

Put the chopped bell pepper, garlic, paprika and olive oil in a blender and pulse until a puree is formed.

Wrap each ham slice around each prawn and transfer to the Air fryer basket.

Cook for about 3 minutes and serve with roasted pepper chutney.

Nutrition:

Calories: 353, Fat: 9.9g, Carbohydrates: 7.6g, Sugar: 1.8g, Protein: 55.4g, Sodium: 904mg

79. Juicy Salmon and Asparagus Parcels

Preparation time: 5 minutes
Cooking time: 13 minutes
Servings: 2
Ingredients:
2 salmon fillets
4 asparagus stalks
¼ cup champagne
Salt and black pepper, to taste
¼ cup white sauce
1 teaspoon olive oil
Directions:
Preheat the Air fryer to 355 o F and grease an Air fryer basket.
Mix all the ingredients in a bowl and divide this mixture evenly over 2 foil papers.
Arrange the foil papers in the Air fryer basket and cook for about 13 minutes.
Dish out in a platter and serve hot.
Nutrition:
Calories: 328, Fat: 16.6g, Carbohydrates: 4.1g, Sugar: 1.8g, Protein: 36.6g, Sodium: 190mg

80. Appetizing Tuna Patties

Preparation time: 15 minutes
Cooking time: 10 minutes
Servings: 6
Ingredients:
2 (6-ounce) cans tuna, drained
½ cup panko bread crumbs
1 egg
2 tablespoons fresh parsley, chopped
2 teaspoons Dijon mustard
Dash of Tabasco sauce
Salt and black pepper, to taste
1 tablespoon fresh lemon juice
1 tablespoon olive oil
Directions:
Preheat the Air fryer to 355 o F and line a baking tray with foil paper.
Mix all the ingredients in a large bowl until well combined.
Make equal sized patties from the mixture and refrigerate overnight.
Arrange the patties on the baking tray and transfer to an Air fryer basket.
Cook for about 10 minutes and dish out to serve warm.
Nutrition:
Calories: 130, Fat: 6.2g, Carbohydrates: 5.1g, Sugar: 0.5g, Protein: 13g, Sodium: 94mg

81. Quick and Easy Shrimp

Preparation time: 10 minutes

Cooking time: 5 minutes
Servings: 2
Ingredients:
½ pound tiger shrimp
1 tablespoon olive oil
½ teaspoon old bay seasoning
¼ teaspoon smoked paprika
¼ teaspoon cayenne pepper
Salt, to taste
Directions:
Preheat the Air fryer to 390 o F and grease an Air fryer basket.
Mix all the ingredients in a large bowl until well combined.
Place the shrimps in the Air fryer basket and cook for about 5 minutes.
Dish out and serve warm.
Nutrition:
Calories: 174, Fat: 8.3g, Carbohydrates: 0.3g, Sugar: 0g, Protein: 23.8g, Sodium: 492mg

82. Crispy Shrimp with Orange Marmalade Dip

Preparation time: 25 minutes
Cooking time: 20 minutes
Servings: 4
Ingredients:
8 large shrimp, peeled and deveined
8 ounces coconut milk
½ cup panko breadcrumbs
Salt and black pepper, to taste
½ teaspoon cayenne pepper
For Dip
½ cup orange marmalade
1 teaspoon mustard
¼ teaspoon hot sauce
1 tablespoon honey
Directions:
Preheat the Air fryer to 350 o F and grease an Air fryer basket.
Mix coconut milk, salt and black pepper in a shallow dish.
Combine breadcrumbs, cayenne pepper, salt and black pepper in another shallow dish.
Coat the shrimps in coconut milk mixture and then roll into the breadcrumb mixture.
Arrange the shrimps in the Air fryer basket and cook for about 20 minutes.
Meanwhile, mix all the dip ingredients and serve with shrimp.
Nutrition:
Calories: 316, Fat: 14.7g, Carbohydrates: 44.3g, Sugar: 31.1g, Protein: 6g, Sodium: 165mg

83. Tuna-Stuffed Potato Boats

Preparation time: 10 minutes
Cooking time: 16 minutes
Servings: 4
Ingredients:
4 starchy potatoes, soaked for about 30 minutes and drain
1 (6-ounce) can tuna, drained
2 tablespoons plain Greek yogurt
1 scallion, chopped and divided
1 tablespoon capers
½ tablespoon olive oil
1 teaspoon red chili powder
Salt and black pepper, to taste
Directions:
Preheat the Air fryer to 355 o F and grease an Air fryer basket.
Arrange the potatoes in the Air fryer basket and cook for about 30 minutes.
Meanwhile, mix tuna, yogurt, red chili powder, salt, black pepper and half of scallion in a bowl and mash the mixture well.
Remove the potatoes from the Air fryer and halve the potatoes lengthwise carefully.
Stuff in the tuna mixture in the potatoes and top with capers and remaining scallion.
Dish out in a platter and serve immediately.
Nutrition:
Calories: 281, Fat: 13g, Carbohydrates: 15.4g, Sugar: 1.8g, Protein: 26.2g, Sodium: 249mg

84. Super-Simple Scallops

Preparation time: 10 minutes
Cooking time: 4 minutes
Servings: 2
Ingredients:
¾ pound sea scallops
1 tablespoon butter, melted
½ tablespoon fresh thyme, minced
Salt and black pepper, to taste
Directions:
Preheat the Air fryer to 390 o F and grease an Air fryer basket.
Mix all the ingredients in a bowl and toss to coat well.
Arrange the scallops in the Air fryer basket and cook for about 4 minutes.
Dish out and serve warm.
Nutrition:
Calories: 202, Fat: 7.1g, Carbohydrates: 4.4g, Sugar: 0g, Protein: 28.7g, Sodium: 315mg

85. Amazing Salmon Fillets

Preparation time: 5 minutes
Cooking time: 7 minutes
Servings: 2
Ingredients:

2 (7-ounce) (¾-inch thick) salmon fillets

1 tablespoon Italian seasoning

1 tablespoon fresh lemon juice

Directions:

Preheat the Air fryer to 355 o F and grease an Air fryer grill pan.

Rub the salmon evenly with Italian seasoning and transfer into the Air fryer grill pan, skin-side up.

Cook for about 7 minutes and squeeze lemon juice on it to serve.

Nutrition:

Calories: 88, Fat: 4.1g, Carbohydrates: 0.1g, Sugar: 0g, Protein: 12.9g, Sodium: 55mg

86. Glazed Halibut Steak

Preparation time: 30 minutes

Cooking time: 11 minutes

Servings: 4

Ingredients:

1 pound haddock steak

1 garlic clove, minced

¼ teaspoon fresh ginger, grated finely

½ cup low-sodium soy sauce

¼ cup fresh orange juice

2 tablespoons lime juice

½ cup cooking wine

¼ cup sugar

¼ teaspoon red pepper flakes, crushed

Directions:

Preheat the Air fryer to 390 o F and grease an Air fryer basket.

Put all the ingredients except haddock steak in a pan and bring to a boil.

Cook for about 4 minutes, stirring continuously and remove from the heat.

Put the haddock steak and half of the marinade in a resealable bag and shake well.

Refrigerate for about 1 hour and reserve the remaining marinade.

Place the haddock steak in the Air fryer basket and cook for about 11 minutes.

Coat with the remaining glaze and serve hot.

Nutrition:

Calories: 219, Fats: 1.1g, Carbohydrates: 17.9g, Sugar: 16.2g, Proteins: 29.7g, Sodium: 1861mg

87. Steamed Salmon with Dill Sauce

Preparation time: 15 minutes

Cooking time: 11 minutes

Servings 2

Ingredients:

1 cup water

2 (6-ounce) salmon fillets

½ cup Greek yogurt

2 tablespoons fresh dill, chopped and divided

2 teaspoons olive oil

Salt, to taste

½ cup sour cream
Directions:
Preheat the Air fryer to 285 o F and grease an Air fryer basket.
Place water the bottom of the Air fryer pan.
Coat salmon with olive oil and season with a pinch of salt.
Arrange the salmon in the Air fryer and cook for about 11 minutes.
Meanwhile, mix remaining ingredients in a bowl to make dill sauce.
Serve the salmon with dill sauce.
Nutrition:
Calories: 224, Fat: 14.4g, Carbohydrates: 3.6g, Sugar: 1.5g, Protein: 21.2g, Sodium: 108mg

Meat Recipes
88. Lime Lamb Mix

Preparation time: 5 minutes
Cooking time: 30 minutes
Servings: 4
Ingredients
2pounds lamb chops
Juice of 1 lime
Zest of 1 lime, grated
A pinch of salt and black pepper
1tablespoon olive oil
1teaspoon sweet paprika
1teaspoon cumin, ground
1tablespoon cumin, ground
Directions
In the air fryer's basket, mix the lamb chops with the lime juice and the other
ingredients, rub and cook at 380 degrees F for 15 minutes on each side.
Serve with a side salad.
Nutrition: Calories 284, Fat 13, Fiber 3, Carbs 5, Protein 15

89. Lamb and Corn

Preparation time: 5 minutes
Cooking time: 30 minutes
Servings: 4
Ingredients
2pounds lamb stew meat, cubed
1cup corn
1cup spring onions, chopped
¼ cup beef stock
1tablespoon olive oil
A pinch of salt and black pepper
2tablespoons rosemary, chopped
Directions
In the air fryer's pan, mix the lamb with the corn, spring onions and the other
ingredients, toss and cook at 380 degrees F for 30 minutes.
Divide the mix between plates and serve.
Nutrition: Calories 274, Fat 12, Fiber 3, Carbs 5, Protein 15

90. Herbed Beef and Squash

Preparation time: 10 minutes
Cooking time: 30 minutes
Servings: 4
Ingredients
2pounds beef stew meat, cubed
1cup butternut squash, peeled and cubed
1tablespoon basil, chopped
1tablespoon oregano, chopped
A pinch of salt and black pepper

A drizzle of olive oil

2garlic cloves, minced

Directions

In the air fryer's pan, mix the beef with the squash and the other ingredients, toss and cook at 380 degrees F for 30 minutes.

Divide between plates and serve.

Nutrition: Calories 284, Fat 13, Fiber 3, Carbs 6, Protein 14

91. Smoked Beef Mix

Preparation time: 5 minutes

Cooking time: 20 minutes

Servings: 4

Ingredients

1pound beef stew meat, roughly cubed

1tablespoon smoked paprika

½ cup beef stock

½ teaspoon garam masala

2tablespoons olive oil

A pinch of salt and black pepper

Directions

In the air fryer's basket, mix the beef with the smoked paprika and the other ingredients, toss and cook at 390 degrees F for 20 minutes on each side.

Divide between plates and serve.

Nutrition: Calories 274, Fat 12, Fiber 4, Carbs 6, Protein 17

92. Marjoram Pork Mix

Preparation time: 5 minutes

Cooking time: 25 minutes

Servings: 4

INGREDIENTS

2pounds pork stew meat, roughly cubed

1tablespoon marjoram, chopped

1cup heavy cream

2tablespoons olive oil

Salt and black pepper to the taste

2garlic cloves, minced

Directions

Heat up a pan that fits the air fryer with the oil over medium-high heat, add the meat and brown for 5 minutes

Add the rest of the ingredients, toss, put the pan in the fryer and cook at 400 degrees F for 20 minutes more.

Divide between plates and serve.

Nutrition: Calories 274, Fat 14, Fiber 3, Carbs 6, Protein 14

93. Nutmeg Lamb

Preparation time: 5 minutes

Cooking time: 30 minutes

Servings: 4

Ingredients

1pound lamb stew meat, cubed
2teaspoons nutmeg, ground
1teaspoon coriander, ground
1cup heavy cream
2tablespoons olive oil
2tablespoons chives, chopped
Salt and black pepper to the taste
DIRECTIONS
In the air fryer's pan, mix the lamb with the nutmeg and the other ingredients, put the pan in the air fryer and cook at 380 degrees F for 30 minutes.
Divide everything into bowls and serve.
Nutrition: Calories 287, Fat 13, Fiber 2, Carbs 6, Protein 12

94. Greek Beef Mix

Preparation time: 5 minutes
Cooking time: 30 minutes
Servings: 4
Ingredients:
2pounds beef stew meat, roughly cubed
1teaspoon coriander, ground
1teaspoon garam masala
1teaspoon cumin, ground
A pinch of salt and black pepper
1cup Greek yogurt
½ teaspoon turmeric powder
DIRECTIONS
In the air fryer's pan, mix the beef with the coriander and the other ingredients, toss and cook at 380 degrees F for 30 minutes.
Divide between plates and serve.
Nutrition: Calories 283, Fat 13, Fiber 3, Carbs 6, Protein 15

95. Beef and Fennel

Preparation time: 5 minutes
Cooking time: 30 minutes
Servings: 4
Ingredients
2pounds beef stew meat, cut into strips
2fennel bulbs, sliced
2tablespoons mustard
A pinch of salt and black pepper
1tablespoon black peppercorns, ground
2tablespoons balsamic vinegar
2tablespoons olive oil
Directions
In the air fryer's pan, mix the beef with the fennel and the other ingredients.
Put the pan in the fryer and cook at 380 degrees for 30 minutes.
Divide everything into bowls and serve.
Nutrition: Calories 283, Fat 13, Fiber 2, Carbs 6, Protein 17

96. Lamb and Eggplant Meatloaf

Preparation time: 5 minutes
Cooking time: 35 minutes
Servings: 4
Ingredients
2pounds lamb stew meat, ground
2eggplants, chopped
1yellow onion, chopped
A pinch of salt and black pepper
½ teaspoon coriander, ground
Cooking spray
2tablespoons cilantro, chopped
1egg
2tablespoons tomato paste
Directions
In a bowl, mix the lamb with the eggplants of the ingredients except the cooking spray and stir.
Grease a loaf pan that fits the air fryer with the cooking spray, add the mix and shape the meatloaf.
Put the pan in the air fryer and cook at 380 degrees F for 35 minutes.
Slice and serve with a side salad.
Nutrition: Calories 263, Fat 12, Fiber 3, Carbs 6, Protein 15

97. Pork Chops with Olives and Corn

Preparation time: 10 minutes
Cooking time: 25 minutes
Servings: 4
Ingredients
2pounds pork chops
1cup kalamata olives, pitted and halved
1cup black olives, pitted and halved
1cup corn
Salt and black pepper to the taste
1tablespoons avocado oil
2tablespoons garlic powder
2tablespoons oregano, dried
Directions
In the air fryer's pan, mix the pork chops with the olives and the other ingredients, toss, cook at 400 degrees F for 25 minutes, divide between plates and serve.
Nutrition: Calories 281, Fat 8, Fiber 7, Carbs 17, Protein 19

98. Beef and Broccoli Mix

Preparation time: 10 minutes
Cooking time: 30 minutes
Servings: 4
Ingredients
1pound beef stew meat, cubed

2cups broccoli florets

½ cup tomato sauce

1teaspoon sweet paprika

2teaspoons olive oil

1tablespoon cilantro, chopped

Directions

In your air fryer, mix the beef with the broccoli and the other ingredients, toss, cook at 390 degrees F for 30 minutes, divide into bowls and serve.

Nutrition: Calories 281, Fat 12, Fiber 7, Carbs 19, Protein 20

99. Cajun Beef Mix

Preparation time: 10 minutes

Cooking time: 30 minutes

Servings: 4

Ingredients

2pounds beef stew meat, cubed

1tablespoon Cajun seasoning

1teaspoon sweet paprika

1teaspoon chili powder

Salt and black pepper to the taste

1tablespoon olive oil

Directions

In a baking dish that fits your air fryer, mix the beef with the seasoning and the other ingredients, toss, introduce the pan in the fryer and cook at 400 degrees F for 30 minutes.

Divide the mix into bowls and serve.

Nutrition: Calories 291, Fat 8, Fiber 7, Carbs 19, Protein 20

100.   Pork with Sprouts and Mushroom Mix

Preparation time: 10 minutes

Cooking time: 30 minutes

Servings: 4

Ingredients

2pounds pork stew meat, cubed

1cup Brussels sprouts, trimmed and halved

1cup mushrooms, sliced

Salt and black pepper to the taste

1tablespoon balsamic vinegar

1yellow onion, chopped

2teaspoons olive oil

Directions

In a baking dish that fits your air fryer, mix the pork with the sprouts and the other ingredients, introduce the pan in the fryer and cook at 390 degrees F for 30 minutes.

Divide everything between plates and serve.

Nutrition: Calories 285, Fat 8, Fiber 2, Carbs 18, Protein 20

101.   Pork Chops and Yogurt Sauce

Preparation time: 10 minutes
Cooking time: 30 minutes
Servings: 4
Ingredients
2tablespoons avocado oil
2pounds pork chops
1cup yogurt
2garlic cloves, minced
1teaspoon turmeric powder
Salt and black pepper to the taste
2tablespoon oregano, chopped
Directions
In the air fryer's pan, mix the pork chops with the yogurt and the other ingredients, toss and cook at 400 degrees F for 30 minutes.
Divide the mix between plates and serve.
Nutrition: Calories 301, Fat 7, Fiber 5, Carbs 19, Protein 22

102.   Lamb and Macadamia Nuts Mix

Preparation time: 10 minutes
Cooking time: 20 minutes
Servings: 4
Ingredients
2pounds lamb stew meat, cubed
2tablespoons macadamia nuts, peeled
1cup baby spinach
½ cup beef stock
2garlic cloves, minced
Salt and black pepper to the taste
1tablespoon oregano, chopped
Directions
In the air fryer's pan, mix the lamb with the nuts and the other ingredients, cook at 380 degrees F for 20 minutes, divide between plates and serve.
Nutrition: Calories 280, Fat 12, Fiber 8, Carbs 20, Protein 19

103.   Beef Rolls

Preparation time: 10 minutes
Cooking time: 14 minutes
Servings: 4
Ingredients:
2 pounds beef steak, opened and flattened with a meat tenderizer
Salt and black pepper to the taste
1 cup baby spinach
3 ounces red bell pepper, roasted and chopped
6 slices provolone cheese
3 tablespoons pesto
Directions:
Arrange flattened beef steak on a cutting board, spread pesto all over, add cheese in a single layer, add bell peppers, spinach, salt and pepper to the taste.

Roll your steak, secure with toothpicks, season again with salt and pepper, place roll in your air fryer's basket and cook at 400 degrees F for 14 minutes, rotating roll halfway.

Leave aside to cool down, cut into 2 inch smaller rolls, arrange on a platter and serve them as an appetizer.

Enjoy!Nutrition:

calories 230, fat 1, fiber 3, carbs 12, protein 10

104.　　Greek Beef Meatballs Salad

Preparation time: 10 minutes
Cooking time: 10 minutes
Servings: 6
Ingredients:
¼ cup milk
17 ounces beef, ground
1 yellow onion, grated
5 bread slices, cubed
1 egg, whisked
¼ cup parsley, chopped
Salt and black pepper to the taste
2 garlic cloves, minced
¼ cup mint, chopped
2 and ½ teaspoons oregano, dried
1 tablespoon olive oil
Cooking spray
7 ounces cherry tomatoes, halved
1 cup baby spinach
1 and ½ tablespoons lemon juice
7 ounces Greek yogurtDirections:
Put torn bread in a bowl, add milk, soak for a few minutes, squeeze and transfer to another bowl.

Add beef, egg, salt, pepper, oregano, mint, parsley, garlic and onion, stir and shape medium meatballs out of this mix.

Spray them with cooking spray, place them in your air fryer and cook at 370 degrees F for 10 minutes.

In a salad bowl, mix spinach with cucumber and tomato.

Add meatballs, the oil, some salt, pepper, lemon juice and yogurt, toss and serve.

Enjoy!Nutrition:

calories 200, fat 4, fiber 8, carbs 13, protein 27

105.　　Beef Patties and Mushroom Sauce

Preparation time: 10 minutes
Cooking time: 25 minutes
Servings: 6
Ingredients:
2 pounds beef, ground
Salt and black pepper to the taste
½ teaspoon garlic powder
1 tablespoon soy sauce

¼ cup beef stock

¾ cup flour

1 tablespoon parsley, chopped

1 tablespoon onion flakes

For the sauce:

1 cup yellow onion, chopped

2 cups mushrooms, sliced

2 tablespoons bacon fat

2 tablespoons butter

½ teaspoon soy sauce

¼ cup sour cream

½ cup beef stock

Salt and black pepper to the tasteDirections:

In a bowl, mix beef with salt, pepper, garlic powder, 1 tablespoon soy sauce, ¼ cup beef stock, flour, parsley and onion flakes, stir well, shape 6 patties, place them in your air fryer and cook at 350 degrees F for 14 minutes.

Meanwhile, heat up a pan with the butter and the bacon fat over medium heat, add mushrooms, stir and cook for 4 minutes.

Add onions, stir and cook for 4 minutes more.

Add ½ teaspoon soy sauce, sour cream and ½ cup stock, stir well, bring to a simmer and take off heat.

Divide beef patties on plates and serve with mushroom sauce on top.

Enjoy!

Nutrition:

calories 435, fat 23, fiber 4, carbs 6, protein 32

106.   Beef Casserole

Preparation time: 30 minutes

Cooking time: 35 minutes

Servings: 12

Ingredients:

1 tablespoon olive oil

2 pounds beef, ground

2 cups eggplant, chopped

Salt and black pepper to the taste

2 teaspoons mustard

2 teaspoons gluten free Worcestershire sauce

28 ounces canned tomatoes, chopped

2 cups mozzarella, grated

16 ounces tomato sauce

2 tablespoons parsley, chopped

1 teaspoon oregano, driedDirections:

In a bowl, mix eggplant with salt, pepper and oil and toss to coat.

In another bowl, mix beef with salt, pepper, mustard and Worcestershire sauce, stir well and spread on the bottom of a pan that fits your air fryer.

Add eggplant mix, tomatoes, tomato sauce, parsley, oregano and sprinkle mozzarella at the end.

Introduce in your air fryer and cook at 360 degrees F for 35 minutes

Divide among plates and serve hot.

Enjoy!

Nutrition:

calories 200, fat 12, fiber 2, carbs 16, protein 15

107.   Lamb and Spinach Mix

Preparation time: 10 minutes

Cooking time: 35 minutes

Servings: 6

Ingredients:

2 tablespoons ginger, grated

2 garlic cloves, minced

2 teaspoons cardamom, ground

1 red onion, chopped

1 pound lamb meat, cubed

2 teaspoons cumin powder

1 teaspoon garam masala

½ teaspoon chili powder

1 teaspoon turmeric

2 teaspoons coriander, ground

1 pound spinach

14 ounces canned tomatoes, choppedDirections:

In a heat proof dish that fits your air fryer, mix lamb with spinach, tomatoes, ginger, garlic, onion, cardamom, cloves, cumin, garam masala, chili, turmeric and coriander, stir, introduce in preheated air fryer and cook at 360 degrees F for 35 minutes

Divide into bowls and serve.

Enjoy!Nutrition:

calories 160, fat 6, fiber 3, carbs 17, protein 20

Side Dish Recipes
108.   Easy Polenta Pie

Preparation time: 10 min
Cooking time: 55 min
Servings: 6
Ingredients:
Egg, slightly beaten (1 piece)
Water (2 cups)
Monterey Jack cheese, w/ jalapeno peppers, shredded (3/4 cup)
Cornmeal (3/4 cup)
Salt (1/4 teaspoon)
Chili beans, drained (15 ounces)
Tortilla chips/crushed corn (1/3 cup)
Directions:
Preheat air fryer at 350 degrees Fahrenheit.
Mist cooking spray onto a pie plate.
In saucepan heated on medium-high, combine water, salt, and cornmeal. Let mixture boil, then cook on medium heat for six minutes. Stir in egg and let sit for five minutes.
Pour cornmeal mixture into pie plate and spread evenly. Air-fry for fifteen minutes and top with beans, corn chips, and cheese. Air-fry for another twenty minutes.
Nutrition: Calories 195 Fat 7.0 g Protein 10.0 g Carbohydrates 27.0 g

109.   Bean and Rice Dish

Preparation time: 10 min
Cooking time: 1 hr 5 min
Servings: 4
Ingredients:
Boiling water (1 ½ cups)
Kidney beans, dark red, undrained (15 ounces)
Marjoram leaves, dried (1/2 teaspoon)
Cheddar cheese, shredded (1/2 cup)
White rice, long grain, uncooked (1 cup)
Bouillon, chicken/vegetable, granulated (1 tablespoon)
Onion, medium, chopped (1 piece)
Baby lima beans, frozen, thawed, drained (9 ounces)
Directions:
Preheat air fryer at 325 degrees Fahrenheit.
Combine all ingredients, save for cheese, in casserole.
Cover and air-fry for one hour and fifteen minutes. Give dish a stir before topping with cheese.
Nutrition: Calories 440 Fat 6.0 g Protein 20.0 g Carbohydrates 77.0 g

110.   Cheesy Potato Mash Casserole

Preparation time: 25 min
Cooking time: 1 hr 10 min
Servings: 24

Ingredients:

Chives, fresh, chopped (1 teaspoon)

Cream cheese, reduced fat, softened (3 ounces)

Yogurt, plain, fat free (1 cup)

Cheddar cheese, reduced fat, shredded (1 cup)

Paprika (1/4 teaspoon)

White potatoes, peeled, cubed (5 pounds)

Blue cheese, crumbled (1/4 cup)

Parmesan cheese, shredded (1/4 cup)

Garlic salt (1 teaspoon)

Directions:

Place potatoes in saucepan filled with water. Heat to boiling, then cook on simmer for fifteen to eighteen minutes.

Beat together parmesan cheese, cheddar cheese, cream cheese, and blue cheese until smooth. Beat in garlic salt and yogurt.

Preheat air fryer t o 325 degrees Fahrenheit.

Mash cooked potatoes until smooth. Stir in cheese mixture. Add to a baking dish and air-fry for thirty-five to forty minutes.

Nutrition: Calories 110 Fat 2.5 g Protein 4.0 g Carbohydrates 18.0 g

111. Simple Squash Casserole

Preparation time: 20 min

Cooking time: 40 min

Servings: 6

Ingredients:

Yellow summer squash, medium, sliced thinly (1 piece)

Thyme leaves, fresh, chopped (1 tablespoon)

Salt (1/2 teaspoon)

Italian cheese blend, gluten free, shredded (1/2 cup)

Olive oil, extra virgin (1 tablespoon)

Zucchini, medium, sliced thinly (1 piece)

Onion, diced (1/2 cup)

Brown rice, cooked (1 cup)

Plum tomato, diced (1 piece)

Pepper (1/8 teaspoon)

Directions:

Preheat air fryer to 375 degrees Fahrenheit.

Mist cooking spray onto a gratin dish.

Combine rice, onion, tomato, pepper, salt (1/4 teaspoon), oil, and ½ thyme leaves. Spread evenly into gratin dish and layer on top with squash and zucchini. Sprinkle with remaining salt (1/4 teaspoon) and thyme.

Cover and air-fry for twenty minutes. Top with cheese and air-fry for another ten to twelve minutes.

Nutrition: Calories 110 Fat 5.0 g Protein 4.0 g Carbohydrates 12.0 g

112. Delicious Ginger Pork Lasagna

Preparation time: 45 min

Cooking time: 45 min

Servings: 8

Ingredients:
Thai basil leaves, fresh, sliced thinly (2 tablespoons)
Butter (1 tablespoon)
Garlic cloves, minced (2 pieces)
Ricotta cheese, part skim (15 ounces)
Wonton wrappers, square (48 pieces)
Green onion greens & whites, separated, sliced thinly (4 pieces)
Fish sauce (1 tablespoon)
Parmesan cheese, shredded (1 tablespoon)
Sesame oil, toasted (1 tablespoon)
Ground pork (1 pound)
Gingerroot, fresh, minced (1 tablespoon)
Tomato sauce (15 ounces)
Chili garlic sauce (1 tablespoon)
Coconut milk (1/2 cup)
Directions:
Preheat air fryer at 325 degrees Fahrenheit.
Mist cooking spray onto a baking dish.
In skillet heated on medium, cook pork in butter and sesame oil for eight to ten minutes. Stir in garlic, green onion whites, and gingerroot and cook for one to two minutes. Stir in fish sauce, chili garlic sauce, and tomato sauce. Cook on gentle simmer.
Combine coconut milk, ricotta cheese, and parmesan cheese (1 cup).
Arrange 8 overlapping wonton wrappers in baking dish to line bottom, then top with a second layer of eight wrappers. Spread on top 1/3 of cheese mixture, and layer with 1/3 of pork mixture. Repeat layering twice and finish by topping with parmesan cheese.
Cover dish with foil and air-fry for thirty minutes. Remove foil and air-fry for another ten to fifteen minutes.
Serve topped with basil and green onion greens.
Nutrition: Calories 480 Fat 24.0 g Protein 28.0 g Carbohydrates 37.0 g

113.   Baked Sweet Potatoes

Preparation time: 10 minutes
Cooking time: 10 minutes
Servings: 2

Ingredients:
2 big sweet potatoes, scrubbed
1 cup water
A pinch of salt and black pepper
½ teaspoon smoked paprika
½ teaspoon cumin, ground

Directions:
Put the water in your pressure cooker, add the steamer basket, add sweet potatoes inside, cover and cook on High for 10 minutes.

Split potatoes, add salt, pepper, paprika and cumin, divide them between plates and serve as a side dish.

Nutrition: calories 152, fat 2, fiber 3, carbs 4, protein 4

114.   Broccoli Pasta

Preparation time: 10 minutes
Cooking time: 4 minutes
Servings: 2
 Ingredients:
2 cups water
½ pound pasta
8 ounces cheddar cheese, grated
½ cup broccoli
½ cup half and half
Directions:
Put the water and the pasta in your pressure cooker.
Add the steamer basket, add the broccoli, cover the cooker and cook on High for 4 minutes.
Drain pasta, transfer it as well as the broccoli, and clean the pot.
Set it on sauté mode, add pasta and broccoli, cheese and half and half, stir well, cook for 2 minutes, divide between plates and serve as a side dish for chicken.

Nutrition: calories 211, fat 4, fiber 2, carbs 6, protein 7

115.   Cauliflower Rice

Preparation time: 10 minutes
Cooking time: 12 minutes
Servings: 2
 Ingredients:
1 tablespoon olive oil
½ cauliflower head, florets separated
A pinch of salt and black pepper
A pinch of parsley flakes
¼ teaspoon cumin, ground
¼ teaspoon turmeric powder
¼ teaspoon paprika
1 cup water
½ tablespoon cilantro, chopped
Juice from 1/3 lime
Directions:
Put the water in your pressure cooker, add the steamer basket, add cauliflower florets, cover and cook on High for 2 minutes.
Discard water, transfer cauliflower to a plate and leave aside.
Clean your pressure cooker, add the oil, set on sauté mode and heat it up.

Add cauliflower, mash using a potato masher, add salt, pepper, parsley, cumin, turmeric, paprika, cilantro and lime juice, stir well, cook for 10 minutes more, divide between 2 plates and serve as a side dish.

Nutrition: calories 191, fat 1, fiber 2, carbs 4, protein 5

116. Refried Beans

Preparation time: 10 minutes
Cooking time: 35 minutes
Servings: 2
Ingredients:
1 pound pinto beans, soaked for 20 minutes and drained
1 cup onion, chopped
2 garlic cloves, minced
1 teaspoon oregano, dried
½ jalapeno, chopped
1 teaspoon cumin, ground
A pinch of salt and black pepper
1 and ½ tablespoon olive oil
2 cups chicken stock

Directions:
In your pressure cooker, mix oil with onion, jalapeno, garlic, oregano, cumin, salt, pepper, stock and beans, stir, cover and cook on Manual for 30 minutes.
Stir beans one more time, divide them between 2 plates and serve as a side dish.
Nutrition: calories 200, fat 1, fiber 3, carbs 7, protein 7

117. Sweet Brussels Sprouts

Preparation time: 10 minutes
Cooking time: 4 minutes
Servings: 2
Ingredients:
½ pounds Brussels sprouts
2 teaspoon buttery spread
½ teaspoon orange zest, grated
1 tablespoon orange juice
½ tablespoon maple syrup
A pinch of salt and black pepper
Directions:
In your pressure cooker, mix Brussels sprouts with buttery spread, orange zest, orange juice, maple syrup, salt and pepper, stir, cover and cook on High for 4 minutes.
Divide between 2 plates and serve as a side dish.

Nutrition: calories 65, fat 2, fiber 3, carbs 10, protein 3

118.   Roasted Potatoes

Preparation time: 10 minutes
Cooking time: 15 minutes
Servings: 2
Ingredients:
½pound potatoes, cut into wedges
¼ teaspoon onion powder
½ teaspoon garlic powder
2 tablespoons avocado oil
A pinch of salt and black pepper
½ cup chicken stock
Directions:
Set your pressure cooker on sauté mode, add the oil and heat it up.
Add potatoes, onion powder, garlic powder, salt and pepper, stir and sauté for 8 minutes.
Add stock, cover and cook on High for 7 minutes more.
Divide between 2 plates and serve as a side dish.

Nutrition: calories 192, fat 1, fiber 4, carbs 8, protein 8

119.   Squash Risotto

Preparation time: 10 minutes
Cooking time: 13 minutes
Servings: 2
Ingredients:
1 small yellow onion, chopped
A drizzle of olive oil
1 garlic clove, minced
½ red bell pepper, chopped
1 cup butternut squash, chopped
1 cup Arborio rice
1 and ½ cups veggie stock
3 tablespoons dry white wine
4 ounces mushrooms, chopped
A pinch of salt and black pepper
A pinch of oregano, dried
¼ teaspoon coriander, ground
1 and ½ cups mixed kale and spinach
1 tablespoon nutritional yeast
Directions:
Set your pressure cooker on sauté mode, add the oil and heat it up.
Add onion, bell pepper, squash and garlic, stir and cook for 5 minutes.
Add rice, stock, wine, salt, pepper, mushrooms, oregano and coriander, stir, cover and cook on High for 5 minutes.

Add mixed kale and spinach, parsley and yeast, stir and leave aside for 5 minutes. Divide between 2 plates and serve as a side dish.

Nutrition: calories 163, fat 1, fiber 2, carbs 3, protein 6

120. Cabbage Side Dish

Preparation time: 10 minutes
Cooking time: 10 minutes
Servings: 2
Ingredients:
½ pound turkey sausage, sliced
½ cabbage head, shredded
2 garlic cloves, minced
½ yellow onion, chopped
1 teaspoon sugar
1 teaspoon balsamic vinegar
1 teaspoon mustard
A drizzle of olive oil
A pinch of salt and black pepper

Directions:
Set your pressure cooker on sauté mode, add the oil and heat it up.
Add onion, sausage and garlic, stir and sauté for 5 minutes.
Add cabbage, sugar, vinegar, mustard, salt and pepper, stir, cover and cook on High for 5 minutes more.
Divide between 2 plates and serve.

Nutrition: calories 200, fat 3, fiber 1, carbs 8, protein 3

121. Beans and Chorizo

Preparation time: 10 minutes
Cooking time: 42 minutes
Servings: 2
Ingredients:
½ tablespoon vegetable oil
3 ounces chorizo, chopped
½ pound black beans
½ yellow onion, chopped
3 garlic cloves, minced
½ orange
1 bay leaf
1 quart chicken stock
A pinch of salt and black pepper
1 tablespoon cilantro, chopped

Directions:

Set your pressure cooker on sauté mode, add the oil and heat it up.
Add chorizo, stir and cook for 2 minutes.
Add garlic, onion, beans, orange, bay leaf, salt, pepper and stock, stir, cover and cook on High for 40 minutes.
Discard bay leaf and orange, add cilantro, stir, divide between plates and serve as a side dish.

Nutrition: calories 224, fat 1, fiber 2, carbs 7, protein 10

122.   Spanish Rice

Preparation time: 10 minutes
Cooking time: 12 minutes
Servings: 2
Ingredients:
½ tablespoon olive oil
½ tablespoon butter
½ cup rice
½ cup chicken stock
½ cup tomato sauce
1 teaspoon chili powder
½ teaspoon cumin, ground
¼ teaspoon oregano, dried
A pinch of salt and black pepper
2 tablespoons tomatoes, chopped

Directions:
Put the oil in your pressure cooker, set on sauté mode and heat it up.
Add rice, stir and cook for 4 minutes.
Add stock, tomato sauce, chili powder, cumin, oregano, tomatoes, salt and pepper, stir, cover and cook on High for 8 minutes.
Stir rice one more time, divide between 2 plates and serve as a side dish.

Nutrition: calories 174, fat 1, fiber 2, carbs 6, protein 8

123.   Spaghetti Squash Delight

Preparation time: 10 minutes
Cooking time: 33 minutes
Servings: 2
Ingredients:
1 cup water
1 small spaghetti squash
½ cup apple juice
1 tablespoon duck fat
A pinch of salt and black pepper
Directions:

Put the water in your pressure cooker, add the steamer basket, add the squash inside, cover and cook on High for 30 minutes.

Cut squash in half, scoop seeds and take out squash spaghetti.

Clean the pressure cooker, set it on sauté mode, add duck fat and heat it up.

Add apple juice, salt and pepper, stir and simmer for 3 minutes.

Divide squash spaghetti between 2 plates, drizzle the sauce all over, toss a bit and serve as a side dish.

Nutrition: calories 183, fat 3, fiber 3, carbs 7, protein 8

124.   Artichokes Side Dish

Preparation time: 10 minutes
Cooking time: 20 minutes
Servings: 2
Ingredients:
2 artichokes, trimmed and tops cut off
1 cup water
1 lemon wedges
Directions:
Rub artichokes with the lemon wedge.

Add the water to your pressure cooker, add the steamer basket, place artichokes inside, cover and cook on High for 20 minutes.

Divide between 2 plates and serve as a side dish.

Nutrition: calories 100, fat 1, fiber 1, carbs 1, protein 3

125.   Cabbage and Cream

Preparation time: 10 minutes
Cooking time: 10 minutes
Servings: 2
Ingredients:
½ cup bacon, chopped
½ yellow onion, chopped
1 cup beef stock
1 pound Savoy cabbage, chopped
A pinch of nutmeg, ground
½ cup coconut milk
1 small bay leaf
1 tablespoon parsley flakes
A pinch of salt
Directions:
Set your pressure cooker on sauté mode, add bacon and onion, stir and cook for 3 minutes.

Add stock, bay leaf and cabbage, cover the cooker and cook on Manual for 4 minutes.

Set the cooker on sauté mode again, add coconut milk, nutmeg and a pinch of salt, discard bay leaf, stir cabbage and simmer for 4 minutes.
Sprinkle parsley flakes at the end, divide between 2 plates and serve.

Nutrition: calories 229, fat 2, fiber 4, carbs 9, protein 6

126.   Carrots and Kale

Preparation time: 10 minutes
Cooking time: 11 minutes
Servings: 2
Ingredients:
10 ounces kale, roughly chopped
1 tablespoon butter
3 carrots, sliced
1 yellow onion, chopped
4 garlic cloves, minced
½ cup chicken stock
A pinch of salt and black pepper
A splash of balsamic vinegar
¼ teaspoon red pepper flakes
Directions:
Set your pressure cooker on sauté mode, add butter and melt it.
Add onion and carrots, stir and cook for 3 minutes.
Add garlic, stir and cook for 1 minute more.
Add kale and stock, cover and cook on High for 7 minutes.
Add vinegar and pepper flakes, stir, divide between 2 plates and serve.

Nutrition: calories 183, fat 2, fiber 3, carbs 6, protein 8

127.   Beets Side Dish

Preparation time: 10 minutes
Cooking time: 25 minutes
Servings: 2
Ingredients:
2 beets
1 tablespoon balsamic vinegar
½ bunch parsley, chopped
A pinch of salt and black pepper
1 small garlic clove, minced
½ tablespoon olive oil
1 tablespoon capers
1 cup water
Directions:
Put the water in your pressure cooker, add the steamer basket, add beets inside, cover and cook on High for 25 minutes.

Transfer beets to a cutting board, leave aside to cool down, peel, slice and transfer to a bowl.

In another bowl, mix parsley with salt, pepper, garlic, oil and capers and whisk really well.

Divide beets on plates, drizzle vinegar all over, add parsley dressing and serve as a side dish.

Nutrition: calories 76, fat 2, fiber 1, carbs 4, protein 1

Dessert Recipes

128.   Fiesta Pastries

Preparation time: 15 minutes
Cooking time: 20 minutes
Servings: 8
Ingredients:
½ of apple, peeled, cored and chopped
1 teaspoon fresh orange zest, grated finely
7.05-ounce prepared frozen puff pastry, cut into 16 squares
½ tablespoon white sugar
½ teaspoon ground cinnamon
Directions:
Preheat the Air fryer to 390 o F and grease an Air fryer basket.
Mix all ingredients in a bowl except puff pastry.
Arrange about 1 teaspoon of this mixture in the center of each square.
Fold each square into a triangle and slightly press the edges with a fork.
Arrange the pastries in the Air fryer basket and cook for about 10 minutes.
Dish out and serve immediately.
Nutrition:
Calories: 147, Fat: 9.5g, Carbohydrates: 13.8g, Sugar: 2.1g, Protein: 1.9g, Sodium: 62mg

129.   Classic Buttermilk Biscuits

Preparation time: 15 minutes
Cooking time: 8 minutes
Servings: 4
Ingredients:
½ cup cake flour
1¼ cups all-purpose flour
¾ teaspoon baking powder
¼ cup + 2 tablespoons butter, cut into cubes
¾ cup buttermilk
1 teaspoon granulated sugar
Salt, to taste
Directions:
Preheat the Air fryer to 400 o F and grease a pie pan lightly.
Sift together flours, baking soda, baking powder, sugar and salt in a large bowl.
Add cold butter and mix until a coarse crumb is formed.
Stir in the buttermilk slowly and mix until a dough is formed.
Press the dough into ½ inch thickness onto a floured surface and cut out circles with a 1¾-inch round cookie cutter.
Arrange the biscuits in a pie pan in a single layer and brush butter on them.
Transfer into the Air fryer and cook for about 8 minutes until golden brown.
Nutrition:
Calories: 374, Fat: 18.2g, Carbohydrates: 45.2g, Sugar: 3.4g, Protein: 7.3g, Sodium: 291mg

130.   Blueberry bowls

Preparation time: 10 minutes
Cooking time: 12 minutes
Servings: 4
Ingredients:
2 cups blueberries
1 cup coconut water
2 tablespoons sugar
2 teaspoons vanilla extract
Juice of ½ lime
Directions:
In your air fryer's pan, combine the blueberries with the water and the other ingredients, toss and cook at 320 degrees f for 12 minutes.
Serve cold.
Nutrition: calories 230, fat 2, fiber 2, carbs 14, protein 7

131.   Carrot brownies

Preparation time: 10 minutes
Cooking time: 25 minutes
Servings: 8
Ingredients:
1 teaspoon almond extract
2 eggs, whisked
½ cup butter, melted
4 tablespoons sugar
2 cups almond flour
½ cup carrot, peeled and grated
Directions:
In a bowl, combine the eggs with the butter and the other ingredients, whisk, spread this into a pan that fits your air fryer, introduce in the fryer and cook at 340 degrees f for 25 minutes.
Cool down, slice and serve.
Nutrition: calories 230, fat 12, fiber 2, carbs 12, protein 5

132.   Yogurt cake

Preparation time: 10 minutes
Cooking time: 30 minutes
Servings: 8
Ingredients:
6 eggs, whisked
1 teaspoon vanilla extract
1 teaspoon baking soda
9 ounces almond flour
4 tablespoons sugar
2 cups yogurt
Directions:

In a blender, combine the eggs with the vanilla and the other ingredients, pulse, spread into a cake pan lined with parchment paper, put it in the air fryer and cook at 330 degrees f for 30 minutes.

Cool the cake down, slice and serve.

Nutrition: calories 231, fat 13, fiber 2, carbs 11, protein 5

133. Chocolate ramekins

Preparation time: 10 minutes
Cooking time: 20 minutes
Servings: 4
Ingredients:
2 cups cream cheese, soft
3 tablespoons sugar
4 eggs, whisked
1 teaspoon vanilla extract
½ cup heavy cream
2 cups white chocolate, melted
Directions:
In a bowl combine the cream cheese with the sugar and the other ingredients, whisk well, divide into 4 ramekins, put them in the air fryer's basket and cook at 370 degrees f for 20 minutes.

Serve cold.

Nutrition: calories 261, fat 12, fiber 6, carbs 12, protein 6

134. Grapes cake

Preparation time: 10 minutes
Cooking time: 25 minutes
Servings: 8
Ingredients:
1 cup coconut flour
1 teaspoon baking powder
¾ teaspoon almond extract
¾ cup sugar
Cooking spray
1 cup heavy cream
2 cup grapes, halved
1 egg, whisked
Directions:
In a bowl, combine the flour with the baking powder and the other ingredients except the cooking spray and whisk well.

Grease a cake pan with cooking spray, pour the cake batter inside, spread, introduce the pan in the air fryer and cook at 330 degrees f for 25 minutes.

Cool the cake down, slice and serve.

Nutrition: calories 214, fat 9, fiber 3, carbs 14, protein 8

135. Carrots bread

Preparation time: 10 minutes
Cooking time: 40 minutes
Servings: 6

Ingredients:

2 cups carrots, peeled and grated

1 cup sugar

3 eggs, whisked

2 cups white flour

1 tablespoon baking soda

1 cup almond milk

Directions:

In a bowl, combine the carrots with the sugar and the other ingredients, whisk well, pour this into a lined loaf pan, introduce the pan in the air fryer and cook at 340 degrees f for 40 minutes.

Cool the bread down, slice and serve.

Nutrition: calories 200, fat 5, fiber 3, carbs 13, protein 7

136.   Pear pudding

Preparation time: 10 minutes

Cooking time: 20 minutes

Servings: 6

Ingredients:

3 tablespoons sugar

½ cup butter, melted

2 eggs, whisked

2 pears, peeled and chopped

1/3 cup almond milk

½ cup heavy cream

Directions:

In a bowl, combine the butter with the sugar and the other ingredients, whisk well and pour into a pudding pan.

Introduce the pan in the air fryer and cook at 340 degrees f for 20 minutes.

Cool the pudding down, divide into bowls and serve.

Nutrition: calories 211, fat 4, fiber 6, carbs 14, protein 6

137.   Lime cake

Preparation time: 10 minutes

Cooking time: 30 minutes

Servings: 4

Ingredients:

1 egg, whisked

2 tablespoons sugar

2 tablespoons butter, melted

½ cup almond milk

2 tablespoons lime juice

1 tablespoon lime zest, grated

1 cup heavy cream

½ teaspoon baking powder

Directions:

In a bowl, combine the egg with the sugar, butter and the other ingredients, whisk well and transfer to a cake pan lined with parchment paper.

Put the pan in your air fryer and cook at 320 degrees f for 30 minutes.

Serve the cake cold.

Nutrition: calories 213, fat 5, fiber 5, carbs 15, protein 6

138.   Pear stew

Preparation time: 10 minutes

Cooking time: 20 minutes

Servings: 4

Ingredients:

2 teaspoons cinnamon powder

4 pears, cored and cut into wedges

1 cup water

2 tablespoons sugar

Directions:

In your air fryer's pan, combine the pears with the water and the other ingredients, cook at 300 degrees f for 20 minutes, divide into cups and serve cold.

Nutrition: calories 200, fat 3, fiber 4, carbs 16, protein 4

139.   Avocado cream

Preparation time: 10 minutes

Cooking time: 10 minutes

Servings: 4

Ingredients:

2 avocados, peeled, pitted and mashed

2 cups heavy cream

2 tablespoons sugar

1 tablespoon lemon juice

Directions:

In a blender, combine the avocados with the cream and the other ingredients, pulse well, divide into 4 ramekins, introduce them in the fryer and cook at 320 degrees f for 10 minutes.

Serve the cream really cold.

Nutrition: calories 171, fat 1, fiber 4, carbs 8, protein 2

140.   Apples and wine sauce

Preparation time: 10 minutes

Cooking time: 20 minutes

Servings: 4

Ingredients:

3 apples, cored and cut intro wedges

1 teaspoon nutmeg, ground

1 cup red wine

½ cup sugar

Directions:

In your air fryer's pan, combine the apples with the nutmeg and the other ingredients, toss and cook at 340 degrees f for 20 minutes.

Divide into bowls and serve.

Nutrition: calories 200, fat 1, fiber 4, carbs 12, protein 3

141.   Mandarin cream

Preparation time: 10 minutes

Cooking time: 15 minutes
Servings: 4
Ingredients:
2 cups heavy cream
2 mandarins, peeled and chopped
1 teaspoon vanilla extract
2 tablespoons sugar
Directions:
In a bowl, combine the cream with the mandarins and the other ingredients, whisk, transfer to 4 ramekins, put them in the air fryer's basket and cook at 300 degrees f for 15 minutes.
Whisk the cream, divide it into cups and serve.
Nutrition: calories 200, fat 3, fiber 4, carbs 11, protein 3

142.   Avocado cake

Preparation time: 10 minutes
Cooking time: 30 minutes
Servings: 4
Ingredients:
2 avocados, peeled, pitted and mashed
1 cup almond flour
2 teaspoons baking powder
1 cup sugar
1 cup butter, melted
3 tablespoons maple syrup
4 eggs, whisked
Directions:
In a bowl, combine the avocados with the flour and the other ingredients, whisk, pour this into a lined cake pan, introduce the pan in the fryer and cook at 340 degrees f for 30 minutes.
Leave the cake to cool down, slice and serve.
Nutrition: calories 213, fat 3, fiber 6, carbs 15, protein 4

143.   Egg pudding

Preparation time: 10 minutes
Cooking time: 25 minutes
Serving: 6
Ingredients:
4 eggs, whisked
1 cup almond milk
½ cup heavy cream
¾ cup sugar
1 teaspoon cinnamon powder
½ teaspoon ginger powder
Directions:
In a bowl, combine the eggs with the almond milk and the other ingredients, whisk, pour into a pudding mould, put it in the air fryer and cook at 340 degrees f for 25 minutes.
Serve the pudding cold.

Nutrition: calories 200, fat 4, fiber 6, carbs 15, protein 4

144.   Quinoa pudding

Preparation time: 10 minutes
Cooking time: 20 minutes
Servings: 6
Ingredients:
2 cups almond milk
1 teaspoon vanilla extract
1 teaspoon nutmeg, ground
1 cup quinoa
½ cup sugar
Directions:
In your air fryer's pan, combine the almond milk with the quinoa and the other ingredients, whisk, and cook at 320 degrees f for 20 minutes.
Divide into bowls and serve.
Nutrition: calories 161, fat 3, fiber 5, carbs 14, protein 4

145.   Cake with cream and strawberries

Preparation time: 10 minutes
Cooking time: 15 minutes
Servings: 2
Ingredients:
1 pure butter puff pastry to stretch
500g strawberries (clean and without skin)
1 bowl of custard
3 tbsp icing sugar baked at 210°C in the air fryer
Direction:
Unroll the puff pastry and place it on the baking sheet. Prick the bottom with a fork and spread the custard. Arrange the strawberries in a circle and sprinkle with icing sugar.
Cook in a fryer setting a 210°C for 15 minutes.
Remove the cake from the fryer with the tongs and let cool.
When serving sprinkle with icing sugar
And why not, add some whipped cream.
Nutrition:
Calories 212.6
Fat 8.3 g
Carbohydrate 31.9 g
Sugars 17.4 g
Protein2.3 g
Cholesterol 21.4 mg

146.   Caramelized Pineapple and Vanilla Ice Cream

Preparation time: 0-10 minutes
Cooking time: 15-30 minutes
Servings: 4
Ingredients:

4 slices Pineapple
20g Butter
50g Cane sugar
Ice cream/vanilla cream
Direction:
Heat the Air Fryer at 1500C for 5 minutes. Let it brown for 15-30 minutes. Then, take it out and top with the cream.
Nutrition:
Calories 648
Fat 36.4g
Carbohydrates 73.2g
Sugar 61.6g
Protein 9.5g
Cholesterol 94mg

147.   Apple Pie

Preparation time: 20-30 minutes
Cooking time: 45-60 minutes
Servings: 3
Ingredients:
600g Flour
350g Margarine
150g Sugar
2 Eggs
50g Breadcrumbs
3 Apples
75g Raisins
75g Sugar
1tsp Cinnamon
Direction:
Put the flour, sugar, eggs, and margarine nuts in the blender just outside the refrigerator.
Mix everything until you get a compact and quite flexible mixture. Let it rest in the refrigerator for at least 30 minutes.
Preheat the air fryer at 1500C for 5 minutes.
Spread 2/3 of the mass of broken dough in 3-4 mm thick covering the previously floured and floured tank and making the edges adhere well, which should be at least 2 cm.
Place the breadcrumbs, apple slices, sugar, raisins, and cinnamon in the bottom; cover everything with the remaining dough and make holes in the top to allow steam to escape.
Cook for 40 minutes and then turn off the lower resistance.
Cook for another 20 minutes only with the upper resistance on. Once it has cooled, put it on a plate and serve.
Nutrition:
Calories 411
Fat 19.38g
Total Carbohydrate 57.5g

Sugars 50g
Protein3.72g
Cholesterol0mg

Vegetarian Recipes

148. Parmesan Broccoli and Asparagus

Preparation Time: 20 minutes
Cooking Time: 15 minutes
Servings: 4
Ingredients:
½ lb. asparagus, trimmed
1 broccoli head, florets separated
Juice of 1 lime
3 tbsp. parmesan, grated
2 tbsp. olive oil
Salt and black pepper to taste.
Directions:
Take a bowl and mix the asparagus with the broccoli and all the other ingredients except the parmesan, toss, transfer to your air fryer's basket and cook at 400°F for 15 minutes
Divide between plates, sprinkle the parmesan on top and serve.
Nutrition: Calories: 172; Fat: 5g; Fiber: 2g; Carbs: 4g; Protein: 9g

149. Italian Asparagus

Preparation Time: 15 minutes
Cooking Time: 10 minutes
Servings: 4
Ingredients:
1 lb. asparagus, trimmed
2 cups cherry tomatoes; halved
2 cups mozzarella, shredded
½ cup balsamic vinegar
2 tbsp. olive oil
A pinch of salt and black pepper
Directions:
In a pan that fits your air fryer, mix the asparagus with the rest of the ingredients except the mozzarella and toss
Put the pan in the air fryer and cook at 400°F for 10 minutes. Divide between plates and serve
Nutrition: Calories: 200; Fat: 6g; Fiber: 2g; Carbs: 3g; Protein: 6g

150. Spinach Cheese Pie

Preparation Time: 10 minutes
Cooking Time: 20 minutes
Servings: 4
Ingredients:
1 cup frozen chopped spinach, drained
¼ cup heavy whipping cream.
1 cup shredded sharp Cheddar cheese.
¼ cup diced yellow onion

6 large eggs.

Directions:

Take a medium bowl, whisk eggs and add cream. Add remaining ingredients to bowl.

Pour into a 6-inch round baking dish. Place into the air fryer basket. Adjust the temperature to 320 Degrees F and set the timer for 20 minutes

Eggs will be firm and slightly browned when cooked. Serve immediately.

Nutrition: Calories: 288; Protein: 18.0g; Fiber: 1.3g; Fat: 20.0g; Carbs: 3.9g

151. Garlic Tomatoes

Preparation Time: 5 minutes

Cooking Time: 15 minutes

Servings: 4

Ingredients:

1 lb. cherry tomatoes; halved

6 garlic cloves; minced

1 tbsp. olive oil

1 tbsp. dill; chopped.

1 tbsp. balsamic vinegar

Salt and black pepper to taste.

Directions:

In a pan that fits the air fryer, combine all the ingredients, toss gently.

Put the pan in the air fryer and cook at 380°F for 15 minutes

Divide between plates and serve.

Nutrition: Calories: 121; Fat: 3g; Fiber: 2g; Carbs: 4g; Protein: 6g

152. Zucchini and Olives

Preparation Time: 5 minutes

Cooking Time: 12 minutes

Servings: 4

Ingredients:

4 zucchinis; sliced

2 tbsp. olive oil

1 cup kalamata olives, pitted

2 tbsp. lime juice

2 tsp. balsamic vinegar

Salt and black pepper to taste.

Directions:

In a pan that fits your air fryer, mix the olives with all the other ingredients, toss, introduce in the fryer and cook at 390°F for 12 minutes

Divide the mix between plates and serve.

Nutrition: Calories: 150; Fat: 4g; Fiber: 2g; Carbs: 4g; Protein: 5g

153. Bacon Asparagus

Preparation Time: 5 minutes

Cooking Time: 10 minutes

Servings: 4

Ingredients:

2 lb. asparagus, trimmed

4 bacon slices, cooked and crumbled
1 cup cheddar cheese, shredded
4 garlic cloves; minced
2 tbsp. olive oil
Directions:
Take a bowl and mix the asparagus with the other ingredients except the bacon, toss and put in your air fryer's basket
Cook at 400°F for 10 minutes, divide between plates, sprinkle the bacon on top and serve.
Nutrition: Calories: 172; Fat: 6g; Fiber: 2g; Carbs: 5g; Protein: 8g

154.   Broccoli and Almonds

Preparation Time: 5 minutes
Cooking Time: 12 minutes
Servings: 4
Ingredients:
1 lb. broccoli florets
½ cup almonds; chopped
3 garlic cloves; minced
1 tbsp. chives; chopped
2 tbsp. red vinegar
3 tbsp. coconut oil; melted
A pinch of salt and black pepper
Directions:
Take a bowl and mix the broccoli with the garlic, salt, pepper, vinegar and the oil and toss.
Put the broccoli in your air fryer's basket and cook at 380°F for 12 minutes
Divide between plates and serve with almonds and chives sprinkled on top.
Nutrition: Calories: 180; Fat: 4g; Fiber: 2g; Carbs: 4g; Protein: 6g

155.   Turmeric Cabbage

Preparation Time: 5 minutes
Cooking Time: 15 minutes
Servings: 4
Ingredients:
1 green cabbage head, shredded
¼ cup ghee; melted
1 tbsp. dill; chopped.
2 tsp. turmeric powder
Directions:
In a pan that fits your air fryer, mix the cabbage with the rest of the ingredients except the dill, toss, put the pan in the fryer and cook at 370°F for 15 minutes
Divide everything between plates and serve with dill sprinkled on top.
Nutrition: Calories: 173; Fat: 5g; Fiber: 3g; Carbs: 6g; Protein: 7g

156.   Parmesan Artichokes

Preparation Time: 10 minutes
Cooking Time: 10 minutes
Servings: 4

Ingredients:

¼ cup blanched finely ground almond flour.

2 medium artichokes, trimmed and quartered, center removed

1 large egg, beaten

½ cup grated vegetarian Parmesan cheese.

2 tbsp. coconut oil

½ tsp. crushed red pepper flakes.

Directions:

Take a large bowl, toss artichokes in coconut oil and then dip each piece into the egg.

Mix the Parmesan and almond flour in a large bowl. Add artichoke pieces and toss to cover as completely as possible, sprinkle with pepper flakes. Place into the air fryer basket

Adjust the temperature to 400 Degrees F and set the timer for 10 minutes. Toss the basket two times during cooking. Serve warm.

Nutrition: Calories: 189; Protein: 7.9g; Fiber: 4.2g; Fat: 13.5g; Carbs: 10.0g

157.   Roasted Broccoli Salad

Preparation Time: 5 minutes

Cooking Time: 10 minutes

Servings: 2

Ingredients:

3 cups fresh broccoli florets.

½ medium lemon.

¼ cup sliced almonds.

2 tbsp. salted butter; melted.

Directions:

Place broccoli into a 6-inch round baking dish. Pour butter over broccoli. Add almonds and toss. Place dish into the air fryer basket

Adjust the temperature to 380 Degrees F and set the timer for 7 minutes. Stir halfway through the cooking time. When timer beeps, zest lemon onto broccoli and squeeze juice into pan. Toss. Serve warm.

Nutrition: Calories: 215; Protein: 6.4g; Fiber: 5.0g; Fat: 16.3g; Carbs: 12.1g

158.   Protein Doughnut Holes

Preparation Time: 10 minutes

Cooking Time: 20 minutes

Servings: 12 holes

Ingredients:

½ cup blanched finely ground almond flour.

1 large egg.

½ cup granular erythritol.

½ cup low-carb vanilla protein powder

½ tsp. baking powder.

5 tbsp. unsalted butter; melted.

½ tsp. vanilla extract.

Directions:

Mix all ingredients in a large bowl. Place into the freezer for 20 minutes.

Wet your hands with water and roll the dough into twelve balls

Cut a piece of parchment to fit your air fryer basket. Working in batches as necessary, place doughnut holes into the air fryer basket on top of parchment Adjust the temperature to 380 Degrees F and set the timer for 6 minutes. Flip doughnut holes halfway through the cooking time. Let cool completely before serving.

Nutrition: Calories: 221; Protein: 19.8g; Fiber: 1.7g; Fat: 14.3g; Carbs: 23.2g

159.   Kale and Bell Peppers

Preparation Time: 5 minutes
Cooking Time: 10 minutes
Servings: 4
Ingredients:
1 ½ cups avocado, peeled, pitted and cubed
2 cups kale, torn
¼ cup olive oil
1 cup red bell pepper; sliced
1 tbsp. white vinegar
2 tbsp. lime juice
1 tbsp. mustard
A pinch of salt and black pepper
Directions:
In a pan that fits the air fryer, combine the kale with salt, pepper, avocado and half of the oil, toss.
Put in your air fryer and cook at 360°F for 10 minutes
In a bowl, combine the kale mix with the rest of the ingredients, toss and serve.
Nutrition: Calories: 131; Fat: 3g; Fiber: 2g; Carbs: 4g; Protein: 5g

160.   Chocolate Chip Pan Cookie

Preparation Time: 10 minutes
Cooking Time: 7 minutes
Servings: 4
Ingredients:
½ cup blanched finely ground almond flour.
1 large egg.
¼ cup powdered erythritol
2 tbsp. unsalted butter; softened.
2 tbsp. low-carb, sugar-free chocolate chips
½ tsp. unflavored gelatin
½ tsp. baking powder.
½ tsp. vanilla extract.
Directions:
Take a large bowl, mix almond flour and erythritol. Stir in butter, egg and gelatin until combined.
Stir in baking powder and vanilla and then fold in chocolate chips
Pour batter into 6-inch round baking pan. Place pan into the air fryer basket.
Adjust the temperature to 300 Degrees F and set the timer for 7 minutes
When fully cooked, the top will be golden brown and a toothpick inserted in center will come out clean. Let cool at least 10 minutes.
Nutrition: Calories: 188; Protein: 5.6g; Fiber: 2.0g; Fat: 15.7g; Carbs: 16.8g

161. Roasted Asparagus

Preparation Time: 15 minutes
Cooking Time: 10 minutes
Servings: 4
Ingredients:
1 lb. asparagus, trimmed
1 tbsp. sweet paprika
3 tbsp. olive oil
A pinch of salt and black pepper
Directions:
Take a bowl and mix the asparagus with the rest of the ingredients and toss
Put the asparagus in your air fryer's basket and cook at 400°F for 10 minutes.
Divide between plates and serve
Nutrition: Calories: 200; Fat: 5g; Fiber: 2g; Carbs: 4g; Protein: 6g

162. Portobello Mini Pizzas

Preparation Time: 5 minutes
Cooking Time: 15 minutes
Servings: 2
Ingredients:
2 large portobello mushrooms
2 leaves fresh basil; chopped
⅔ cup shredded mozzarella cheese
4 grape tomatoes, sliced
1 tbsp. balsamic vinegar
2 tbsp. unsalted butter; melted.
½ tsp. garlic powder.
Directions:
Scoop out the inside of the mushrooms, leaving just the caps. Brush each cap with butter and sprinkle with garlic powder.
Fill each cap with mozzarella and sliced tomatoes. Place each mini pizza into a 6-inch round baking pan. Place pan into the air fryer basket.
Adjust the temperature to 380 Degrees F and set the timer for 10 minutes
Carefully remove the pizzas from the fryer basket and garnish with basil and a drizzle of vinegar.
Nutrition: Calories: 244; Protein: 10.4g; Fiber: 1.4g; Fat: 18.5g; Carbs: 6.8g

163. Frying Potatoes

Preparation time: 5 minutes
Cooking time: 40 minutes
Servings: 4
Ingredients:
5 to 6 medium potatoes
Olive oil in a spray bottle if possible
Mill salt
Freshly ground pepper
 Direction:
Wash the potatoes well and dry them.

Brush with a little oil on both sides if not with the oil

Crush some ground salt and pepper on top.

Place the potatoes in the fryer basket

Set the cooking at 190°C for 40 minutes, in the middle of cooking turn the potatoes for even cooking on both sides.

At the end of cooking, remove the potatoes from the basket, cut them in half and slightly scrape the melting potato inside and add only a little butter, and enjoy!

Nutrition:

Calories 365

Fat 17g

Carbohydrates 48g

Sugars 0.3g

Protein 4g

Cholesterol 0mg

164.   Avocado Fries

Preparation time: 5 minutes

Cooking time: 10 minutes

Serving: 1

Ingredients:

1 egg

1 ripe avocado

½ tsp salt

½ cup of panko breadcrumbs

Direction:

Preheat the air fryer to 400°F (200°C) for 5 minutes.

Remove the avocado pit and cut into fries. In a small bowl, whisk the egg with the salt.

Enter the breadcrumbs on a plate.

Dip the quarters in the egg mixture, then in the breadcrumbs.

Put them in the fryer. Cook for 8-10 minutes.

Turn halfway through cooking.

Nutrition:

Calories 390

Fat 32g

Carbohydrates 24g

Sugars 3g

Protein 4g

Cholesterol 0mg

165.   Crispy French Fries

Preparation time: 5 minutes; Cooking time: 10 minutes; Serve: 2

Ingredients:

2 medium sweet potatoes

2 tsp olive oil

½ tsp salt

½ tsp garlic powder

¼ tsp paprika

Black pepper

Direction:

Preheat the hot air fryer to 400°F (200°C)

Spray the basket with a little oil.

Cut the sweet potatoes into potato chips about 1 cm wide.

Add oil, salt, garlic powder, pepper and paprika.

Cook for 8 minutes, without overloading the basket.

Repeat 2 or 3 times, as necessary.

Nutrition:

Calories 240

Fat 9g

Carbohydrates 36g

Sugars 1g

Protein 3g

Cholesterol 0mg

166.   Frying Potatoes with Butter

Preparation time: 5 minutes

Cooking time: 10 minutes

Servings: 2

Ingredients:

2 Russet potatoes

Butter

Fresh parsley (optional)

Direction:

Spray the basket with a little oil.

Open your potatoes along.

Make some holes with a fork.

Add the butter and parsley.

Transfer to the basket. If your air fryer to a temperature of 198°C (390°F).

Cook for 30 to 40 minutes.

Try about 30 minutes. Bon Appetite!

Nutrition:

Calories 365

Fat 17g

Carbohydrates 48g

Sugars 0.3g

Protein 4g

Cholesterol 0mg

167.   Homemade French Fries

Preparation time: 5 minutes

Cooking time: 10 minutes

Servings: 2

Ingredients:

2.5 lb. sliced and sliced potato chips

1 tbsp olive oil

Salt and pepper to taste

1 tsp salt to season or paprika

Direction:

Put the fries in a bowl with very cold water.
Let it soak for at least 30 minutes.
Drain completely. Add the oil. Shake
Put them in the fryer bowl. Cook for 15 to 25 minutes. Set to 380°F (193°C).
Set the time according to your preferences or the power of your fryer to 23
minutes.
Nutrition:
Calories 118
Fat 7g
Carbohydrates 27
Sugars 1g
Protein 2
Cholesterol 0mg

Brunch Recipes
168.   Radish Hash Browns

Preparation Time: 10 minutes
Cooking Time: 13 minutes
Servings: 4
Ingredients:
1 lb radishes, washed and cut off roots
1 tbsp olive oil
1/2 tsp paprika
1/2 tsp onion powder
1/2 tsp garlic powder
1 medium onion
1/4 tsp pepper
3/4 tsp sea salt
Directions:
Slice onion and radishes using a mandolin slicer.
Add sliced onion and radishes in a large mixing bowl and toss with olive oil.
Transfer onion and radish slices in air fryer basket and cook at 360 F for 8 minutes. Shake basket twice.
Return onion and radish slices in a mixing bowl and toss with seasonings.
Again, cook onion and radish slices in air fryer basket for 5 minutes at 400 F.
Shake basket halfway through.
Serve and enjoy.
Nutrition:
Calories 62
Fat 3.7 g
Carbohydrates 7.1 g
Sugar 3.5 g
Protein 1.2 g
Cholesterol 0 mg

169.   Vegetable Egg Cups

Preparation Time:10 minutes
Cooking Time:20 minutes
Servings:4
Ingredients:
4 eggs
1 tbsp cilantro, chopped
4 tbsp half and half
1 cup cheddar cheese, shredded
1 cup vegetables, diced
Pepper
Salt
Directions:
Spray four ramekins with cooking spray and set aside.
In a mixing bowl, whisk eggs with cilantro, half and half, vegetables, 1/2 cup cheese, pepper, and salt.

Pour egg mixture into the four ramekins.

Place ramekins in air fryer basket and cook at 300 F for 12 minutes.

Top with remaining 1/2 cup cheese and cook for 2 minutes more at 400 F.

Serve and enjoy.

Nutrition:

Calories 194

Fat 11.5 g

Carbohydrates 6 g

Sugar 0.5 g

Protein 13 g

Cholesterol 190 mg

170. Spinach Frittata

Preparation Time: 5 minutes

Cooking Time: 8 minutes

Servings: 1

Ingredients:

3 eggs

1 cup spinach, chopped

1 small onion, minced

2 tbsp mozzarella cheese, grated

Pepper

Salt

Directions:

Preheat the air fryer to 350 F.

Spray air fryer pan with cooking spray.

In a bowl, whisk eggs with remaining ingredients until well combined.

Pour egg mixture into the prepared pan and place pan in the air fryer basket.

Cook frittata for 8 minutes or until set.

Serve and enjoy.

Nutrition:

Calories 384

Fat 23.3 g

Carbohydrates 10.7 g

Sugar 4.1 g

Protein 34.3 g

Cholesterol 521 mg

171. Omelette Frittata

Preparation Time: 10 minutes

Cooking Time: 6 minutes

Servings: 2

Ingredients:

3 eggs, lightly beaten

2 tbsp cheddar cheese, shredded

2 tbsp heavy cream

2 mushrooms, sliced

1/4 small onion, chopped

1/4 bell pepper, diced

Pepper
Salt
Directions:
In a bowl, whisk eggs with cream, vegetables, pepper, and salt.
Preheat the air fryer to 400 F.
Pour egg mixture into the air fryer pan. Place pan in air fryer basket and cook for 5 minutes.
Add shredded cheese on top of the frittata and cook for 1 minute more.
Serve and enjoy.
Nutrition:
Calories 160
Fat 10 g
Carbohydrates 4 g
Sugar 2 g
Protein 12 g
Cholesterol 255 mg

172.   Cheese Soufflés

Preparation Time: 10 minutes
Cooking Time: 6 minutes
Servings: 8
Ingredients:
6 large eggs, separated
3/4 cup heavy cream
1/4 tsp cayenne pepper
1/2 tsp xanthan gum
1/2 tsp pepper
1/4 tsp cream of tartar
2 tbsp chives, chopped
2 cups cheddar cheese, shredded
1 tsp salt
Directions:
Preheat the air fryer to 325 F.
Spray eight ramekins with cooking spray. Set aside.
In a bowl, whisk together almond flour, cayenne pepper, pepper, salt, and xanthan gum.
Slowly add heavy cream and mix to combine.
Whisk in egg yolks, chives, and cheese until well combined.
In a large bowl, add egg whites and cream of tartar and beat until stiff peaks form.
Fold egg white mixture into the almond flour mixture until combined.
Pour mixture into the prepared ramekins. Divide ramekins in batches.
Place the first batch of ramekins into the air fryer basket.
Cook soufflé for 20 minutes.
Serve and enjoy.
Nutrition:
Calories 210
Fat 16 g

Carbohydrates 1 g
Sugar 0.5 g
Protein 12 g
Cholesterol 185 mg

173.   Simple Egg Soufflé

Preparation Time: 5 minutes
Cooking Time: 8 minutes
Servings: 2
Ingredients:
2 eggs
1/4 tsp chili pepper
2 tbsp heavy cream
1/4 tsp pepper
1 tbsp parsley, chopped
Salt
Directions:
In a bowl, whisk eggs with remaining gradients.
Spray two ramekins with cooking spray.
Pour egg mixture into the prepared ramekins and place into the air fryer basket.
Cook soufflé at 390 F for 8 minutes.
Serve and enjoy.
Nutrition:
Calories 116
Fat 10 g
Carbohydrates 1.1 g
Sugar 0.4 g
Protein 6 g
Cholesterol 184 mg

174.   Vegetable Egg Soufflé

Preparation Time: 10 minutes
Cooking Time: 20 minutes
Servings: 4
Ingredients:
4 large eggs
1 tsp onion powder
1 tsp garlic powder
1 tsp red pepper, crushed
1/2 cup broccoli florets, chopped
1/2 cup mushrooms, chopped
Directions:
Spray four ramekins with cooking spray and set aside.
In a bowl, whisk eggs with onion powder, garlic powder, and red pepper.
Add mushrooms and broccoli and stir well.
Pour egg mixture into the prepared ramekins and place ramekins into the air fryer basket.
Cook at 350 F for 15 minutes. Make sure souffle is cooked if souffle is not cooked then cook for 5 minutes more.

Serve and enjoy.
Nutrition:
Calories 91
Fat 5.1 g
Carbohydrates 4.7 g
Sugar 2.6 g
Protein 7.4 g
Cholesterol 186 mg

175. Asparagus Frittata

Preparation Time: 10 minutes
Cooking Time: 10 minutes
Servings: 4
Ingredients:
6 eggs
3 mushrooms, sliced
10 asparagus, chopped
1/4 cup half and half
2 tsp butter, melted
1 cup mozzarella cheese, shredded
1 tsp pepper
1 tsp salt
Directions:
Toss mushrooms and asparagus with melted butter and add into the air fryer basket.
Cook mushrooms and asparagus at 350 F for 5 minutes. Shake basket twice.
Meanwhile, in a bowl, whisk together eggs, half and half, pepper, and salt.
Transfer cook mushrooms and asparagus into the air fryer baking dish.
Pour egg mixture over mushrooms and asparagus.
Place dish in the air fryer and cook at 350 F for 5 minutes or until eggs are set.
Slice and serve.
Nutrition:
Calories 211
Fat 13 g
Carbohydrates 4 g
Sugar 1 g
Protein 16 g
Cholesterol 272 mg

176. Spicy Cauliflower Rice

Preparation Time: 10 minutes
Cooking Time: 22 minutes
Servings: 2
Ingredients:
1 cauliflower head, cut into florets
1/2 tsp cumin
1/2 tsp chili powder
6 onion spring, chopped
2 jalapenos, chopped

4 tbsp olive oil

1 zucchini, trimmed and cut into cubes

1/2 tsp paprika

1/2 tsp garlic powder

1/2 tsp cayenne pepper

1/2 tsp pepper

1/2 tsp salt

Directions:

Preheat the air fryer to 370 F.

Add cauliflower florets into the food processor and process until it looks like rice.

Transfer cauliflower rice into the air fryer baking pan and drizzle with half oil.

Place pan in the air fryer and cook for 12 minutes, stir halfway through.

Heat remaining oil in a small pan over medium heat.

Add zucchini and cook for 5-8 minutes.

Add onion and jalapenos and cook for 5 minutes.

Add spices and stir well. Set aside.

Add cauliflower rice in the zucchini mixture and stir well.

Serve and enjoy.

Nutrition:

Calories 254

Fat 28 g

Carbohydrates 12.3 g

Sugar 5 g

Protein 4.3 g

Cholesterol 0 mg

177. Broccoli Stuffed Peppers

Preparation Time: 10 minutes

Cooking Time: 40 minutes

Servings: 2

Ingredients:

4 eggs

1/2 cup cheddar cheese, grated

2 bell peppers, cut in half and remove seeds

1/2 tsp garlic powder

1 tsp dried thyme

1/4 cup feta cheese, crumbled

1/2 cup broccoli, cooked

1/4 tsp pepper

1/2 tsp salt

Directions:

Preheat the air fryer to 325 F.

Stuff feta and broccoli into the bell peppers halved.

Beat egg in a bowl with seasoning and pour egg mixture into the pepper halved over feta and broccoli.

Place bell pepper halved into the air fryer basket and cook for 35-40 minutes.

Top with grated cheddar cheese and cook until cheese melted.

Serve and enjoy.

Nutrition:
Calories 340
Fat 22 g
Carbohydrates 12 g
Sugar 8.2 g
Protein 22 g
Cholesterol 374 mg

178. Zucchini Muffins

Preparation Time: 10 minutes
Cooking Time: 20 minutes
Servings: 8
Ingredients:
6 eggs
4 drops stevia
1/4 cup Swerve
1/3 cup coconut oil, melted
1 cup zucchini, grated
3/4 cup coconut flour
1/4 tsp ground nutmeg
1 tsp ground cinnamon
1/2 tsp baking soda
Directions:
Preheat the air fryer to 325 F.
Add all ingredients except zucchini in a bowl and mix well.
Add zucchini and stir well.
Pour batter into the silicone muffin molds and place into the air fryer basket.
Cook muffins for 20 minutes.
Serve and enjoy.
Nutrition:
Calories 136
Fat 12 g
Carbohydrates 1 g
Sugar 0.6 g
Protein 4 g
Cholesterol 123 mg

179. Jalapeno Breakfast Muffins

Preparation Time: 10 minutes
Cooking Time: 15 minutes
Servings: 8
Ingredients:
5 eggs
1/3 cup coconut oil, melted
2 tsp baking powder
3 tbsp erythritol
3 tbsp jalapenos, sliced
1/4 cup unsweetened coconut milk
2/3 cup coconut flour

3/4 tsp sea salt
Directions:
Preheat the air fryer to 325 F.
In a large bowl, stir together coconut flour, baking powder, erythritol, and sea salt.
Stir in eggs, jalapenos, coconut milk, and coconut oil until well combined.
Pour batter into the silicone muffin molds and place into the air fryer basket.
Cook muffins for 15 minutes.
Serve and enjoy.
Nutrition:
Calories 125
Fat 12 g
Carbohydrates 7 g
Sugar 6 g
Protein 3 g
Cholesterol 102 mg

180.   Zucchini Noodles

Preparation Time: 10 minutes
Cooking Time: 44 minutes
Servings: 3
Ingredients:
1 egg
1/2 cup parmesan cheese, grated
1/2 cup feta cheese, crumbled
1 tbsp thyme
1 garlic clove, chopped
1 onion, chopped
2 medium zucchinis, trimmed and spiralized
2 tbsp olive oil
1 cup mozzarella cheese, grated
1/2 tsp pepper
1/2 tsp salt
Directions:
Preheat the air fryer to 350 F.
Add spiralized zucchini and salt in a colander and set aside for 10 minutes.
Wash zucchini noodles and pat dry with a paper towel.
Heat oil in a pan over medium heat.
Add garlic and onion and sauté for 3-4 minutes.
Add zucchini noodles and cook for 4-5 minutes or until softened.
Add zucchini mixture into the air fryer baking pan. Add egg, thyme, cheeses. Mix well and season.
Place pan in the air fryer and cook for 30-35 minutes.
Serve and enjoy.
Nutrition:
Calories 435
Fat 29 g
Carbohydrates 10.4 g

Sugar 5 g

Protein 25 g

Cholesterol 120 mg

181.   Mushroom Frittata

Preparation Time: 10 minutes

Cooking Time: 13 minutes

Servings: 1

Ingredients:

1 cup egg whites

1 cup spinach, chopped

2 mushrooms, sliced

2 tbsp parmesan cheese, grated

Salt

Directions:

Spray pan with cooking spray and heat over medium heat.

Add mushrooms and sauté for 2-3 minutes. Add spinach and cook for 1-2 minutes or until wilted.

Transfer mushroom spinach mixture into the air fryer pan.

Whisk egg whites in a mixing bowl until frothy. Season with a pinch of salt.

Pour egg white mixture into the spinach and mushroom mixture and sprinkle with parmesan cheese.

Place pan in air fryer basket and cook frittata at 350 F for 8 minutes.

Slice and serve.

Nutrition:

Calories 176

Fat 3 g

Carbohydrates 4 g

Sugar 2.5 g

Protein 31 g

Cholesterol 8 mg

182.   Egg Muffins

Preparation Time: 10 minutes

Cooking Time: 15 minutes

Servings: 12

Ingredients:

9 eggs

1/2 cup onion, sliced

1 tbsp olive oil

8 oz ground sausage

1/4 cup coconut milk

1/2 tsp oregano

1 1/2 cups spinach

3/4 cup bell peppers, chopped

Pepper

Salt

Directions:

Preheat the air fryer to 325 F.

Add ground sausage in a pan and sauté over medium heat for 5 minutes.
Add olive oil, oregano, bell pepper, and onion and sauté until onion is translucent.
Add spinach to the pan and cook for 30 seconds.
Remove pan from heat and set aside.
In a mixing bowl, whisk together eggs, coconut milk, pepper, and salt until well beaten.
Add sausage and vegetable mixture into the egg mixture and mix well.
Pour egg mixture into the silicone muffin molds and place into the air fryer basket. (Cook in batches)
Cook muffins for 15 minutes.
Serve and enjoy.
Nutrition:
Calories 135
Fat 11 g
Carbohydrates 1.5 g
Sugar 1 g
Protein 8 g
Cholesterol 140 mg

183.   Potato Omelet

Preparation time: 15 minutes
Cooking time: 20 minutes
Servings: 4
Ingredients:
1 ½ potatoes; cubed
1 yellow onion; chopped.
2 tsp. olive oil
2 eggs
1/2 tsp. thyme; dried
1 green bell pepper; chopped
Salt and black pepper to the taste
Directions:
Heat up your air fryer at 350 degrees F; add oil, heat it up, add onion, bell pepper, salt and pepper; stir and cook for 5 minutes.
Add potatoes, thyme and eggs, stir, cover and cook at 360 °F, for 20 minutes.
Divide among plates and serve for breakfast.
Nutrition:
Calories: 241; Fat: 4; Fiber: 7; Carbs: 12; Protein: 7

184.   Veggie Mix

Preparation time: 10 Minutes
Cooking time: 25 minutes
Servings: 6
Ingredients:
1 yellow onion; sliced
1 red bell pepper; chopped.
1 gold potato; chopped.
2 tbsp. olive oil

8 eggs

2 tbsp. mustard

3 cups milk

8 oz. brie; trimmed and cubed

12 oz. sourdough bread; cubed

4 oz. parmesan; grated

Salt and black pepper to the taste

Directions:

Heat up your air fryer at 350 degrees F; add oil, onion, potato and bell pepper and cook for 5 minutes.

In a bowl; mix eggs with milk, salt, pepper and mustard and whisk well.

Add bread and brie to your air fryer; Add the vegetables and seasoning mixture. Add the rest of the bread and parmesan; toss just a little bit and cook for 20 minutes.

Divide among plates and serve for breakfast.

Nutrition:

Calories: 231; Fat: 5; Fiber: 10; Carbs: 20; Protein: 12

185. Special Corn Flakes Casserole

Preparation time: 10 Minutes

Cooking time: 8minutes

Servings: 5

Ingredients:

1/3 cup milk

4 tbsp. cream cheese; whipped

1/4 tsp. nutmeg; ground

1/4 cup blueberries

1 ½ cups corn flakes; crumbled

3 tsp. sugar

2 eggs; whisked

5 bread slices

Directions:

In a bowl; mix eggs with sugar, nutmeg and milk and whisk well.

In another bowl; mix cream cheese with blueberries and whisk well.

Put corn flakes in a third bowl.

Spread blueberry mix on each bread slice; then dip in eggs mix and dredge in corn flakes at the end.

Place bread in your air fryer's basket; heat up at 400 °F and bake for 8 minutes.

Divide among plates and serve for breakfast.

Nutrition:

Calories: 300; Fat: 5; Fiber: 7; Carbs: 16; Protein: 4

186. Broccoli Quiches

Preparation time: 10 Minutes

Cooking time: 20 minutes

Servings: 2

Ingredients:

1 broccoli head; florets separated and steamed

1 tomato; chopped.

1 tsp. thyme; chopped
1 carrots; chopped and steamed
2 oz. cheddar cheese; grated
2 oz. milk
1 tsp. parsley; chopped
2 eggs
Salt and black pepper to the taste
Directions:
In a bowl; mix eggs with milk, parsley, thyme, salt and pepper and whisk well.
Put broccoli, carrots and tomato in your air fryer.
Add eggs mix on top, spread cheddar cheese; cover and cook at 350 °F, for 20 minutes. Divide among plates and serve for breakfast.
Nutrition:
Calories: 214; Fat: 4; Fiber: 7; Carbs: 12; Protein: 3

187.   Spinach Parcels

Preparation time: 10 Minutes
Cooking time: 4 minutes
Servings: 2
Ingredients:
1 lb. baby spinach leaves; roughly chopped
4 sheets filo pastry
1/2 lb. ricotta cheese
2 tbsp. pine nuts
1 eggs; whisked
Zest from 1 lemon; grated
Greek yogurt for serving
Salt and black pepper to the taste
Directions:
In a bowl; mix spinach with cheese, egg, lemon zest, salt, pepper and pine nuts and stir.
Arrange filo sheets on a working surface, divide spinach mix; fold diagonally to shape your parcels and place them in your preheated air fryer at 400 degrees F.
Bake parcels for 4 minutes; divide them on plates and serve them with Greek yogurt on the side.
Nutrition:
Calories: 182; Fat: 4; Fiber: 8; Carbs: 9; Protein: 5

The Best Recipes Ever
188.   Turkey Rolls
Preparation Time: 20 minutes
Cooking Time: 40 minutes
Servings: 3
Ingredients
1 pound turkey breast fillet
1 garlic clove, crushed
1½ teaspoons ground cumin
1 teaspoon ground cinnamon
½ teaspoon red chili powder
Salt, to taste
2 tablespoons olive oil
3 tablespoons fresh parsley, finely chopped
1 small red onion, finely chopped
Directions
Place the turkey fillet on a cutting board.
Carefully, cut horizontally along the length about 1/3 of way from the top, stopping about ¼-inch from the edge.
Open this part to have a long piece of fillet.
In a bowl, mix together the garlic, spices, and oil.
In a small cup, reserve about 1 tablespoon of oil mixture.
In the remaining oil mixture, add the parsley, and onion and mix well.
Set the temperature of Air Fryer to 355 degrees F. Grease an Air Fryer basket.
Coat the open side of fillet with onion mixture.
Roll the fillet tightly from the short side.
With a kitchen string, tie the roll at 1-1½-inch intervals.
Coat the outer side of roll with the reserved oil mixture.
Arrange roll into the prepared Air Fryer basket.
Air Fry for about 40 minutes.
Remove from Air Fryer and place the turkey roll onto a cutting board for about 5-10 minutes before slicing.
With a sharp knife, cut the turkey roll into desired size slices and serve.
Nutrition:
Calories: 239
Carbohydrate: 3.2g
Protein: 37.5g
Fat: 8.2g
Sugar: 0.9g
Sodium: 46mg
189.   Turkey Meatloaf
Preparation Time: 20 minutes
Cooking Time: 20 minutes
Servings: 4
Ingredients
1 pound ground turkey

1 cup kale leaves, trimmed and finely chopped

1 cup onion, chopped

1 (4-ounces) can chopped green chilies

2 garlic cloves, minced

1 egg, beaten

½ cup fresh breadcrumbs

1 cup Monterey Jack cheese, grated

¼ cup salsa verde

3 tablespoons chopped fresh cilantro

1 teaspoon red chili powder

½ teaspoon ground cumin

½ teaspoon dried oregano, crushed

Salt and ground black pepper, as required

Directions

In a deep bowl, put all the ingredients and with your hands, mix until well combined.

Divide the turkey mixture into 4 equal-sized portions and shape each into a mini loaf.

Set the temperature of air fryer to 400 degrees F. Grease an air fryer basket.

Arrange loaves into the prepared air fryer basket.

Air fry for about 20 minutes.

Remove from air fryer and place the loaves onto plates for about 5 minutes before serving.

Serve warm.

Nutrition:

Calories: 435

Carbohydrate: 18.1g

Protein: 42.2g

Fat: 23.1g

Sugar: 3.6g

Sodium: 641mg

190.   Buttered Duck Breasts

Preparation Time: 15 minutes

Cooking Time: 22 minutes

Servings: 4

Ingredients

2 (12-ounces) duck breasts

Salt and ground black pepper, as required

3 tablespoons unsalted butter, melted

½ teaspoon dried thyme, crushed

¼ teaspoon star anise powder

Directions

With a sharp knife, score the fat of duck breasts several times.

Season the duck breasts generously with salt and black pepper.

Set the temperature of Air Fryer to 390 degrees F. Grease an Air Fryer basket.

Arrange duck breasts into the prepared Air Fryer basket.

Air Fry for about 10 minutes.

Remove duck breasts from the basket and coat with melted butter and sprinkle with thyme and star anise powder.

Place duck breasts into the Air Fryer basket for the second time.

Air Fry for about 12 more minutes.

Remove from Air Fryer and place the duck breasts onto a cutting board for about 5-10 minutes before slicing.

Using a sharp knife, cut each duck breast into desired size slices and serve.

Nutrition:

Calories: 296

Carbohydrate: 0.1g

Protein: 37.5g

Fat: 15.5g

Sugar: 0g

Sodium: 100mg

191. **Beer Coated Duck Breast**

Preparation Time: 15 minutes

Cooking Time: 20 minutes

Servings: 2 servings

Ingredients

1 tablespoon olive oil

1 teaspoon mustard

1 tablespoon fresh thyme, chopped

1 cup beer

Salt and ground black pepper, as required

1 (10½-ounces) duck breast

6 cherry tomatoes

1 tablespoon balsamic vinegar

Directions

In a bowl, mix together the oil, mustard, thyme, beer, salt, and black pepper.

Add the duck breast and generously coat with marinade.

Cover and refrigerate for about 4 hours.

Set the temperature of Air Fryer to 390 degrees F.

With a piece of foil, cover the duck breast and arrange into an Air Fryer basket.

Air Fry for about 15 minutes.

Remove the foil from breast.

Now, set the temperature of Air Fryer to 355 degrees F. Grease the Air Fryer basket.

Place duck breast and tomatoes into the prepared Air Fryer basket.

Air Fry for about 5 minutes.

Remove from Air Fryer and place the duck breast onto a cutting board for about 5 minutes before slicing.

With a sharp knife, cut the duck breast into desired size slices and transfer onto serving plates.

Drizzle with vinegar and serve alongside the cherry tomatoes.

Nutrition

Calories: 332

Carbohydrate: 9.2g

Protein: 34.6g
Fat: 13.7g
Sugar: 2.5g
Sodium: 88mg

192.   Duck Breast with Figs

Prep Time: 20 minutes
Cooking Time: 45 minutes
Servings: 2
Ingredients
2 cups fresh pomegranate juice
2 tablespoons lemon juice
3 tablespoons brown sugar
1 pound boneless duck breast
6 fresh figs, halved
1 teaspoon olive oil
Salt and ground black pepper, as required
1 tablespoon fresh thyme, chopped
Directions
In a medium saucepan, add the pomegranate juice, lemon juice, and brown sugar over medium heat and bring to a boil.
Now, lower the heat to low and cook for about 25 minutes until the mixture becomes thick.
Remove the pan from heat and let it cool slightly.
Set the temperature of Air Fryer to 400 degrees F. Grease an Air Fryer basket.
Score the fat of duck breasts several times using a sharp knife.
Sprinkle the duck breast with salt and black pepper.
Arrange duck breast into the prepared Air Fryer basket, skin side up.
Air Fry for about 14 minutes, flipping once halfway through.
Remove from Air Fryer and place the duck breast onto a cutting board for about 5-10 minutes.
Meanwhile, in a bowl, add the figs, oil, salt, and black pepper and toss to coat well.
 Once again, set the temperature of Air Fryer to 400 degrees F. Grease the Air Fryer basket.
Arrange figs into the prepared basket in a single layer.
Air Fry for about 5 minutes.
Using a sharp knife, cut the duck breast into desired size slices and transfer onto serving plates alongside the roasted figs.
Drizzle with warm pomegranate juice mixture and serve with the garnishing of fresh thyme.
Nutrition:
Calories: 669
Carbohydrate: 90g
Protein: 519g
Fat: 12.1g
Sugar: 74g
Sodium: 110mg

193.   Herbed Duck Legs

Preparation Time: 10 minutes
Cooking Time: 30 minutes
Servings: 2
Ingredients
1 garlic clove, minced
½ tablespoon fresh thyme, chopped
½ tablespoon fresh parsley, chopped
1 teaspoon five spice powder
Salt and ground black pepper, as required
2 duck legs
Directions
Set the temperature of air fryer to 340 degrees F. Grease an air fryer basket.
In a bowl, mix together the garlic, herbs, five spice powder, salt, and black pepper.
Generously rub the duck legs with garlic mixture.
Arrange duck legs into the prepared air fryer basket.
Air fry for about 25 minutes and then 5 more minutes at 390 degrees F.
Remove from air fryer and place the duck legs onto the serving platter.
Serve hot.
Nutrition
Calories: 138
Carbohydrate: 1g
Protein: 25g
Fat: 4.5g
Sugar: 0g
Sodium: 82mg

194.   Easy Rib Eye Steak

Preparation Time: 10 minutes
Cooking Time: 14 minutes
 Servings: 4
Ingredients
2 lbs. rib eye steak
1 tablespoon olive oil
1 tablespoon steak rub*
Directions
Set the temperature of air fryer to 400 degrees F. Grease an air fryer basket.
Coat the steak with oil and then, generously rub with steak rub.
Place steak into the prepared air fryer basket.
Air fry for about 14 minutes, flipping once halfway through.
Remove from air fryer and place the steak onto a cutting board for about 10 minutes before slicing.
Cut the steak into desired size slices and transfer onto serving plates.
Serve immediately.
Nutrition
Calories: 438
Carbohydrate: 0g

Protein: 26.88g
Fat: 35.8g
Sugar: 0g
Sodium: 157mg

195. Buttered Striploin Steak

Servings: 2
Prep Time: 10 minutes
Cooking Time: 12 minutes
Ingredients
2 (7-ounces) striploin steak
1½ tablespoons butter, softened
Salt and ground black pepper, as required
Directions
Coat each steak evenly with butter and then, season with salt and black pepper.
Set the temperature of air fryer to 392 degrees F. Grease an air fryer basket.
Arrange steaks into the prepared air fryer basket.
Air fry for about 8-12 minutes.
Remove from air fryer and transfer the steaks onto serving plates.
Serve hot.
Nutrition
Calories: 595
Carbohydrate: 0g
Protein: 58.1g
Fat: 37.6g
Sugar: 0g
Sodium: 452mg

196. Simple New York Strip Steak

Prep Time: 10 minutes
Cooking Time: 8 minutes
Servings: 2
Ingredients
1 (9½-ounces) New York strip steak
Kosher salt and ground black pepper, as required
1 teaspoon olive oil
Directions
Set the temperature of air fryer to 400 degrees F. Grease an air fryer basket.
Coat the steak with oil and then, generously season with salt and black pepper.
Place steak into the prepared air fryer basket.
Air fry for about 7-8 minutes or until desired doneness.
Remove from air fryer and place the steak onto a cutting board for about 10 minutes before slicing.
Cut the steak into desired size slices and transfer onto serving plates.
Serve immediately.
Nutrition:
Calories: 186
Carbohydrate: 0g
Protein: 30.2g

Fat: 7g
Sugar: 0g
Sodium: 177mg

197.   Crispy Sirloin Steak

Preparation Time: 15 minutes
Cooking Time: 10 minutes
Servings: 2 servings
Ingredients
1 cup white flour
2 eggs
1 cup panko breadcrumbs
1 teaspoon garlic powder
1 teaspoon onion powder
Salt and ground black pepper, as required
2 (6-ounces) sirloin steaks, pounded
Directions
In a shallow bowl, place the flour.
Crack the eggs in a second bowl and beat well.
In a third bowl, mix together the panko and spices.
Coat each steak with the white flour, then dip into beaten eggs and finally, coat with panko mixture.
Set the temperature of air fryer to 360 degrees F. Grease an air fryer basket.
Arrange steaks into the prepared air fryer basket.
Air fry for about 10 minutes.
Remove from air fryer and transfer the steaks onto the serving plates.
Serve immediately.
Nutrition:
Calories: 561
Carbohydrate: 6.1g
Protein: 31.9g
Fat: 50.3g
Sugar: 0.6g
Sodium: 100mg

198.   Spiced & Herbed Skirt Steak

Preparation Time: 15 minutes
Cooking Time: 10 minutes
 Servings: 4
Ingredients
3 garlic cloves, minced
1 cup fresh parsley leaves, finely chopped
3 tablespoons fresh oregano, finely chopped
3 tablespoons fresh mint leaves, finely chopped
1 tablespoon ground cumin
2 teaspoons smoked paprika
1 teaspoon cayenne pepper
1 teaspoon red pepper flakes, crushed
Salt and ground black pepper, as required

¾ cup olive oil

3 tablespoons red wine vinegar

2 (8-ounces) skirt steaks

Directions

In a bowl, mix together the garlic, herbs, spices, oil, and vinegar.

In a resealable bag, place ¼ cup of the herb mixture and steaks.

Seal the bag and shake to coat well.

Refrigerate for about 24 hours.

Reserve the remaining herb mixture in refrigerator.

Take out the steaks from fridge and place at room temperature for about 30 minutes.

Set the temperature of air fryer to 390 degrees F. Grease an air fryer basket.

Arrange steaks into the prepared air fryer basket.

Air fry for about 8-10 minutes.

Remove from air fryer and place the steaks onto a cutting board for about 10 minutes before slicing.

Cut each steak into desired size slices and transfer onto serving platter.

Top with reserved herb mixture and serve.

Nutrition:

Calories: 561

Carbohydrate: 6.1g

Protein: 31.9g

Fat: 50.3g

Sugar: 0.6g

Sodium: 100mg

199.   Skirt Steak with Veggies

Servings: 4

Preparation Time: 15 minutes

Cooking Time: 6 minutes

Ingredients

¼ cup olive oil, divided

2 tablespoons soy sauce

2 tablespoons honey

1 (12-ounces) skirt steak, cut into thin strips

½ pound fresh mushrooms, quartered

6 ounces snow peas

1 onion, cut into half rings

Salt and ground black pepper, as required

Directions

In a bowl, mix together 2 tablespoons of oil, soy sauce, and honey.

Add the steak strips and generously coat with the oil mixture.

In another bowl, add the vegetables, remaining oil, salt, and black pepper. Toss to coat well.

Set the temperature of air fryer to 390 degrees F. Grease an air fryer basket.

Arrange steak strips and vegetables into the prepared air fryer basket.

Air fry for about 5-6 minutes or until desired doneness.

Remove from air fryer and place the steak onto a cutting board for about 10 minutes before slicing.

Cut each steak into desired size slices and transfer onto serving plates.

Serve immediately alongside the veggies.

Nutrition:

Calories: 360

Carbohydrate: 16.7g

Protein: 26.7g

Fat: 21.5g

Sugar: 12.6g

Sodium: 522mg

200.   Steak with Bell Peppers

Servings: 4

Preparation Time: 20 minutes

Cooking Time: 22 minutes

Ingredients

1 teaspoon dried oregano, crushed

1 teaspoon onion powder

1 teaspoon garlic powder

1 teaspoon red chili powder

1 teaspoon paprika

Salt, to taste

1¼ pounds beef steak, cut into thin strips

2 green bell peppers, seeded and cubed

1 red bell pepper, seeded and cubed

1 red onion, sliced

2 tablespoons olive oil

Directions

In a large bowl, mix together the oregano and spices.

Add the beef strips, bell peppers, onion, and oil. Mix until well combined.

Set the temperature of air fryer to 390 degrees F. Grease an air fryer basket.

Arrange steak strips mixture into the prepared Air Fryer basket in 2 batches.

Air Fry for about 10-11 minutes or until done completely.

Remove from air fryer and transfer the steak mixture onto serving plates.

Serve immediately.

Nutrition:

Calories: 372

Carbohydrate: 11.2g

Protein: 44.6g

Fat: 16.3g

Sugar: 6.2g

Sodium: 143mg

201.   Buttered Filet Mignon

Servings: 4 servings

Preparation Time: 10 minutes

Cooking Time: 14 minutes)

Ingredients

2 (6-ounces) filet mignon steaks
1 tablespoon butter, softened
Salt and ground black pepper, as required
Directions
Coat each steak evenly with butter and then, season with salt and black pepper.
Set the temperature of air fryer to 390 degrees F. Grease an air fryer basket.
Arrange steaks into the prepared air fryer basket.
Air fry for about 14 minutes, flipping once halfway through.
Remove from the air fryer and transfer onto serving plates.
Serve hot.
Nutrition:
Calories: 403
Carbohydrate: 0g
Protein: 48.7g
Fat: 22g
Sugar: 0g
Sodium: 228mg

202. Bacon Wrapped Filet Mignon

Servings: 2 servings
Preparation Time: 15 minutes
Cooking Time: 15 minutes
Ingredients
2 bacon slices
2 (6-ounces) filet mignon steaks
Salt and ground black pepper, as required
1 teaspoon avocado oil
Directions
Wrap 1 bacon slice around each mignon steak and secure with a toothpick.
Season the steak evenly with salt and black pepper.
Then, coat each steak with avocado oil.
Set the temperature of air fryer to 375 degrees F. Grease an air fryer basket.
Arrange steaks into the prepared air fryer basket.
Air fry for about 15 minutes, flipping once halfway through.
Remove from air fryer and transfer the steaks onto serving plates.
Serve hot.
Nutrition:
Calories: 512
Carbohydrate: 0.5g
Protein: 59.4g
Fat: 28.6g
Sugar: 0g
Sodium: 857mg

203. Crispy Salt and Pepper Tofu

Preparation Time: 5 Minutes
Cooking Time: 15 Minutes
Servings: 4
Ingredients:

¼ cup chickpea flour

¼ cup arrowroot (or cornstarch)

1 teaspoon sea salt

1 teaspoon granulated garlic

½ teaspoon freshly grated black pepper

1 (15-ounce) package tofu, firm or extra-firm

Cooking oil spray (sunflower, safflower, or refined coconut)

Asian Spicy Sweet Sauce, optional

Directions:

1.In a medium bowl, combine the flour, arrowroot, salt, garlic, and pepper. Stir well to combine.

2.Cut the tofu into cubes (no need to press—if it's a bit watery, that's fine!). Place the cubes into the flour mixture. Toss well to coat. Spray the tofu with oil and toss again. (The spray will help the coating better stick to the tofu.)

3.Spray the air fryer basket with the oil. Place the tofu in a single layer in the air fryer basket (you may have to do this in 2 batches, depending on the size of your appliance) and spray the tops with oil. Fry for 8 minutes. Remove the air fryer basket and spray again with oil. Toss gently or turn the pieces over. Spray with oil again and fry for another 7 minutes, or until golden-browned and very crisp.

4.Serve immediately, either plain or with the Asian Spicy Sweet Sauce.

Nutrition: Calories 148; Total fat: 5g; Saturated fat: 0g; Cholesterol: 0mg; Sodium: 473mg; Carbohydrates: 14g; Fiber: 1g; Protein: 11g

204.   Crispy Indian Wrap

Preparation Time: 20 Minutes

Cook Time: 8 Minutes

Servings: 4

Ingredients:

Cilantro Chutney

2¾ cups diced potato, cooked until tender

2 teaspoons oil (coconut, sunflower, or safflower)

3 large garlic cloves, minced or pressed

1½ tablespoons fresh lime juice

1½ teaspoons cumin powder

1 teaspoon onion granules

1 teaspoon coriander powder

½ teaspoon sea salt

½ teaspoon turmeric

¼ teaspoon cayenne powder

4 large flour tortillas, preferably whole grain or sprouted

1 cup cooked garbanzo beans (canned are fine), rinsed and drained

½ cup finely chopped cabbage

¼ cup minced red onion or scallion

Cooking oil spray (sunflower, safflower, or refined coconut)

Directions:

1.Make the Cilantro Chutney and set aside.

2.In a large bowl, mash the potatoes well, using a potato masher or large fork. Add the oil, garlic, lime, cumin, onion, coriander, salt, turmeric, and cayenne. Stir very well, until thoroughly combined. Set aside.

3.Lay the tortillas out flat on the counter. In the middle of each, evenly distribute the potato filling. Add some of the garbanzo beans, cabbage, and red onion to each, on top of the potatoes.

4.Spray the air fryer basket with oil and set aside. Enclose the Indian wraps by folding the bottom of the tortillas up and over the filling, then folding the sides in—and finally rolling the bottom up to form, essentially, an enclosed burrito.

5.Place the wraps in the air fryer basket, seam side down. They can touch each other a little bit, but if they're too crowded, you'll need to cook them in batches. Fry for 5 minutes. Spray with oil again, flip over, and cook an additional 2 or 3 minutes, until nicely browned and crisp. Serve topped with the Cilantro Chutney.

I find that Ezekiel brand sprouted whole-grain tortillas usually break when you try to wrap them. So I always seek out Alvarado Street Bakery brand, since they're much less likely to break on me!

Nutrition: Calories: 288; Total fat: 7g; Saturated fat: 1g; Cholesterol: 0mg; Sodium: 821mg; Carbohydrates: 50g; Fiber: 5g; Protein: 9g

205.   Easy Peasy Pizza

Preparation Time: 5 Minutes
Cooking Time: 9 Minutes
Servings: 1
Ingredients:
Cooking oil spray (coconut, sunflower, or safflower)
1 flour tortilla, preferably sprouted or whole grain
¼ cup vegan pizza or marinara sauce
⅓ cup grated vegan mozzarella cheese or Cheesy Sauce
Toppings of your choice
Directions:

1.Spray the air fryer basket with oil. Place the tortilla in the air fryer basket. If the tortilla is a little bigger than the base, no probs! Simply fold the edges up a bit to form a semblance of a "crust."

2.Pour the sauce in the center, and evenly distribute it around the tortilla "crust" (I like to use the back of a spoon for this purpose).

3.Sprinkle evenly with vegan cheese, and add your toppings. Bake for 9 minutes, or until nicely browned. Remove carefully, cut into four pieces, and enjoy.

For a gluten-free version, use a brown rice tortilla. Create a Mexican pizza with Cheesy Sauce and black beans—and then top with fresh tomatoes, cilantro, red onions, and a little Green Chili Sauce. You can even air-fry the tortilla by itself until crisp and browned, and then top with hummus, spinach, basil, Kalamata olives, and tomatoes for a Greek-inspired pizza. Get creative and have fun!

Nutrition: Calories: 210; Total fat: 6g; Saturated fat: 1g; Cholesterol: 0mg; Sodium: 700mg; Carbohydrates: 33g; Fiber: 2g; Protein: 5g

206.   Eggplant Parmigiana

Preparation Time: 15 Minutes
Cooking Time: 40 Minutes

Servings: 4

Ingredients:

1 medium eggplant (about 1 pound), sliced into ½-inch-thick rounds

2 tablespoons tamari or shoyu

3 tablespoons nondairy milk, plain and unsweetened

1 cup chickpea flour (see Substitution Tip)

1 tablespoon dried basil

1 tablespoon dried oregano

2 teaspoons garlic granules

2 teaspoons onion granules

½ teaspoon sea salt

½ teaspoon freshly ground black pepper

Cooking oil spray (sunflower, safflower, or refined coconut)

Vegan marinara sauce (your choice)

Shredded vegan cheese (preferably mozzarella; see Ingredient Tip)

Directions:

1. Place the eggplant slices in a large bowl, and pour the tamari and milk over the top. Turn the pieces over to coat them as evenly as possible with the liquids. Set aside.

2. Make the coating: In a medium bowl, combine the flour, basil, oregano, garlic, onion, salt, and pepper and stir well. Set aside.

3. Spray the air fryer basket with oil and set aside.

4. Stir the eggplant slices again and transfer them to a plate (stacking is fine). Do not discard the liquid in the bowl.

5. Bread the eggplant by tossing an eggplant round in the flour mixture. Then, dip in the liquid again. Double up on the coating by placing the eggplant again in the flour mixture, making sure that all sides are nicely breaded. Place in the air fryer basket.

6. Repeat with enough eggplant rounds to make a (mostly) single layer in the air fryer basket. (You'll need to cook it in batches, so that you don't have too much overlap and it cooks perfectly.)

7. Spray the tops of the eggplant with enough oil so that you no longer see dry patches in the coating. Fry for 8 minutes. Remove the air fryer basket and spray the tops again. Turn each piece over, again taking care not to overlap the rounds too much. Spray the tops with oil, again making sure that no dry patches remain. Fry for another 8 minutes, or until nicely browned and crisp.

8. Repeat steps 5 to 7 one more time, or until all of the eggplant is crisp and browned.

9. Finally, place half of the eggplant in a 6-inch round, 2-inch deep baking pan and top with marinara sauce and a sprinkle of vegan cheese. Fry for 3 minutes, or until the sauce is hot and cheese is melted (be careful not to overcook, or the eggplant edges will burn). Serve immediately, plain or over pasta. Otherwise, you can store the eggplant in the fridge for several days and then make a fresh batch whenever the mood strikes by repeating this step!

If you're not into chickpea flour (or are dying to make this and don't have it on hand), feel free to try an equal amount of another type of flour. Some that might work well include brown rice flour, whole-wheat pastry, or regular unbleached

white. I personally like the chickpea flour here because of its nutritional profile and hearty consistency, but you may prefer another variety, and that's okay!
I haven't found a whole-food substitute for vegan mozzarella that works quite as well in this dish; if you prefer not to use packaged vegan cheese, simply omit.
Nutrition: Calories: 217; Total fat: 9g; Saturated fat: 1g; Cholesterol: 0mg; Sodium: 903mg; Carbohydrates: 38g; Fiber: 10g; Protein: 9g

207.   Luscious Lazy Lasagna

Preparation Time: 15 Minutes
Cooking Time: 15 Minutes
Servings: 4
Ingredients:
8 ounces lasagna noodles, preferably bean-based, but any kind will do
1 tablespoon extra-virgin olive oil
2 cups crumbled extra-firm tofu, drained and water squeezed out
2 cups loosely packed fresh spinach
2 tablespoons nutritional yeast
2 tablespoons fresh lemon juice
1 teaspoon onion granules
1 teaspoon sea salt
⅛ teaspoon freshly ground black pepper
4 large garlic cloves, minced or pressed
2 cups vegan pasta sauce, your choice
½ cup shredded vegan cheese (preferably mozzarella)
Directions:
1.Cook the noodles until a little firmer than al dente (they'll get a little softer after you air-fry them in the lasagna). Drain and set aside.
2.While the noodles are cooking, make the filling. In a large pan over medium-high heat, add the olive oil, tofu, and spinach. Stir-fry for a minute, then add the nutritional yeast, lemon juice, onion, salt, pepper, and garlic. Stir well and cook just until the spinach is nicely wilted. Remove from heat.
3.To make half a batch (one 6-inch round, 2-inch deep baking pan) of lasagna: Spread a thin layer of pasta sauce in the baking pan. Layer 2 or 3 lasagna noodles on top of the sauce. Top with a little more sauce and some of the tofu mixture. Place another 2 or 3 noodles on top, and add another layer of sauce and then another layer of tofu. Finish with a layer of noodles, and then a final layer of sauce. Sprinkle about half of the vegan cheese on top (omit if you prefer; see the Ingredient Tip from the Eggplant Parmigiana).
4.Place the pan in the air fryer and bake for 15 minutes, or until the noodles are browning around the edges and the cheese is melted. Cut and serve.
5.If making the entire recipe now, repeat steps 3 and 4 (see Cooking Tip).
Please note that you'll need to make this recipe in two batches. If you're serving four people all at once, you'll want to repeat steps 3 and 4 once your first batch is done. However, if you're only serving one or two people when you make this, you'll prepare a second lasagna for another day after cooking your first batch. In that case, layer up your second lasagna as outlined in step 3 and then store it in the fridge (covered) for up to 4 or 5 days, and air-fry it whenever you're ready for another fresh-from-the-"oven" batch.

Nutrition: Calories: 317; Total fat: 8g; Saturated fat: 1g; Cholesterol: 0mg; Sodium: 1203mg; Carbohydrates: 46g; Fiber: 4g; Protein: 20g

Conclusion

I hope this Air Fryer Cookbook helps you understand the dynamics and principles of this revolutionary kitchen appliance, why you should use it and how it's going to change your outlook on food preparation and healthy living.

The next step is to get into the right frame of mind and decide that it's time to take charge of your eating habits by only putting the best organic and free range ingredients in your Air Fryer.

Even if you have never tried the Air Fryer before, I can promise you one thing, after the 30 days, you will be kicking yourself for having not discovered this sooner.

I hope it was able to inspire you to clean up your kitchen from all the useless appliances that clutter your countertop and start putting the Air Fryer to good use.

The Air Fryer is definitely a change in lifestyle that will make things much easier for you and your family. You'll discover increased energy, decreased hunger, a boosted metabolism and of course a LOT more free time!

Happy Air Frying!